'What kind of place makes us creative? Adrian Mourby has examined the rooms where thoughts and characters were born that still resonate across the ages. A fascinating study.'
Julian Fellowes

'[Adrian Mourby's books are] indispensible holiday companions.' *Monocle* magazine

'Homes do influence and reflect their occupants – and no more so than our literary greats who once soaked up the atmosphere, or just sat and sucked their pencils, studied the cracks or the wall paper … This is Adrian Mourby's subject in his new book *Rooms of One's Own.*' Hunter Davies

'A fine selection of quick essays concerning where great writers wrote.' *Bookbag*

'A valuable little book that should really be treasured for providing huge amounts of insight without the reader having to go anywhere at all.' *The Page Printed*

'Adrian Mourby has a delightful way about him. His writing is warm and characterful.' *Outlet*

'Insightful and beautifully packaged.' *Bookwitty*

'This is a lovely little book to sit down with and fly around the world from your armchair.' *Butterfly Elephant*

Rooms of One's Own

50 Places that Made Literary History

ADRIAN MOURBY

This edition published in the UK in 2018 by
Icon Books Ltd, Omnibus Business Centre,
39–41 North Road, London N7 9DP
email: info@iconbooks.com
www.iconbooks.com

Previously published in the UK in
2017 by Icon Books Ltd

Sold in the UK, Europe and Asia
by Faber & Faber Ltd, Bloomsbury House,
74–77 Great Russell Street,
London WC1B 3DA or their agents

Distributed in the UK, Europe and Asia
by Grantham Book Services, Trent Road,
Grantham NG31 7XQ

Distributed in the USA by
Publishers Group West,
1700 Fourth Street, Berkeley, CA 94710

Distributed in Canada by Publishers Group Canada,
76 Stafford Street, Unit 300,
Toronto, Ontario M6J 2S1

Distributed in Australia and New Zealand
by Allen & Unwin Pty Ltd,
PO Box 8500, 83 Alexander Street,
Crows Nest, NSW 2065

Distributed in South Africa by
Jonathan Ball, Office B4, The District,
41 Sir Lowry Road, Woodstock 7925

ISBN: 978-178578-338-8

Typesetting by Simmons Pugh

Printed and bound in the UK by Clays Ltd, St Ives plc

To my wife Kate
Companion for fifteen years of these travels

Adrian Mourby was an award-winning BBC drama producer before turning to full-time writing. He has published three novels, two AA travel guides and a book of humour based on his Sony Award-winning Radio 4 series *Whatever Happened To...?* In recent years Adrian has won two Italian awards for his travel journalism. He also writes extensively on opera and has produced operas by Mozart, Handel and Purcell, both in the UK and in Europe.

AUTHOR'S NOTE

Many of the places visited in this book are open to the general public. Some are in private hands with no right of access. Others are operated by bodies like the National Trust. Some took many approaches before access was agreed. It's always best to make contact well in advance before visiting, and of course sometimes you will have to accept no for answer.

CONTENTS

London

Oxford

Edinburgh

Channel Islands

Paris

Berlin

New York & New Orleans

St Petersburg

East Asia

North Africa

INTRODUCTION

Virginia Woolf famously said that, if she is to write fiction, 'a woman must have money and a room of her own'.

This book explores how male and female writers have over the last two centuries found rooms that inspired them to write, from Tennessee Williams' garret in New Orleans to the room with a view that E.M. Forster coveted in Florence.

En route I was able discover something of Damon Runyon's New York, Graham Greene's Saigon, and George Sand's Venice.

Not every great writer or every room that has witnessed great literature has made it into these 50 chapters. This was very much a personal quest in pursuit of writers who interested me and I didn't want to spend too much time in birthplaces that have been turned into well-meaning museums.

For some of the authors in this book, sitting in the right room was all-important. Marcel Proust's housekeeper claimed that having to relocate from the apartment where he began *À la recherche du temps perdu* exacerbated his ill-health and hastened his death, leaving that ambitious novel sequence incomplete. Victor Hugo spent a fortune turning his house on Guernsey into a very personal Hugo theme park.

For other writers the room can become a location in their fiction. H.G. Wells set one of his bestselling works, *Mr Britling Sees It Through*, in his own house in Essex. Olivia Manning used her own Cairo flat in the Levant Trilogy. But others had no need for their subject matter to be in front of them. James Joyce wrote exclusively about Dublin while sitting in his favourite Paris restaurants.

Over the last few years I've visited rooms where the author's presence is almost palpable in the arrangement of every individual object, and others that seem to bear no relationship to the author or the work produced there.

Some writers have preferred to work in a favourite café – J.K. Rowling is only a recent example in a line that stretches back well beyond Sartre. Oscar Wilde liked to write and entertain in expensive hotels but Hemingway and Noël Coward stayed in the best hotels around the world simply because they could. They could write well regardless of their surroundings.

I've also followed my writers into pubs, apartments, holiday cottages and homes that are now literary museums.

There are some surprises along the way: young Norman Mailer, staying in his parents' apartment, trying to have a conversation by the mailboxes with the diffident playwright who lived downstairs and concluding that Arthur Miller could go to hell; Erich Maria Remarque locked in the bathroom by Marlene Dietrich when the Nazis came to visit; a delirious Somerset Maugham overhearing the manageress of his hotel asking the doctor to remove him to hospital as a death would be bad for business.

This book consists of 50 literary pilgrimages – to London, Oxford, Paris, Berlin and St Petersburg, as well as to Italy, America, North Africa and the Far East. I didn't just want to write about writers beavering away in the family's spare room so I followed many on their travels – because writers do love to travel. Sometimes they are seeking the ideal place in which to work, sometimes they are escaping from life at home. Often they are travelling because their success makes it possible and they know all they need is a pen and paper – or laptop – to continue writing and so they seize on invitations with alacrity.

There is always something to be learned when you visit the place where a book was written. Sometimes the location features directly in what ends up on the page, but more often than not it's significantly altered. We expect writers to be good at their craft and we like them to be inspired by their surroundings, but we can't expect them to be honest as well.

Adrian Mourby, 2017

ROOMS OF ONE'S OWN

ITALY

HOTEL DANIELI, VENICE – GEORGE SAND (1804–76)

I arrived in Venice one chilly January many years ago when the Adriatic was seeping, slowly but relentlessly, across Riva degli Schiavoni. It was exactly 160 years previously that Amantine-Lucile-Aurore Dupin picked her way along this quayside. It wasn't difficult to discover her story. She is commemorated by an inscription within a particular bedroom in Venice's first commercial hotel.

Aurore Dupin was one of Hotel Danieli's earliest celebrity guests. When she arrived in January 1834 she was trailing scandal and her new lover, the poet Alfred de Musset.

Today Aurore is better known as George Sand, a pen name she adopted in her twenties, just as she adopted masculine attire and male smoking habits. At the age of 27 she left her husband and entered upon a four-year period of rebellion that included affairs with prominent writers and the production of a large number of books. That same year, 1831, she published her first novel, *Rose et Blanche*, written in collaboration with her then-lover Jules Sandeau, but for her next novel *Indiana* (1832) she adopted the pen name George Sand. By 1833 Sand had moved on to an affair with the young poet and dramatist Alfred de Musset.

Seven years older than the 23-year-old poet, Sand was keen that they should travel together to Italy where she wished to set her next book. This meant leaving behind her

Photo: Aixabay

two children (aged five and ten) but the novelist was more concerned with getting the blessing of de Musset's mother for their journey. The two women met in Sand's carriage outside Mme de Musset's Paris home. Evidently *Maman* was overwhelmed by Sand's eloquence and promises to take great care of the young man.

The couple took a carriage from Paris to Marseille where they boarded a steamer to Livorno, arriving in January 1834 to a very grey Venice. They took a suite of rooms at the Danieli in what is now Room 10, overlooking Riva degli Schiavoni.

By the time the lovers had unpacked, their six-month romance was cooling. On the journey south Sand had shocked de Musset by her conversation, regaling other passengers with the fact that she was born within a month of her parents' marriage, and with steamy stories of her mother's affairs during the Napoleonic Wars. George Sand courted outrage.

In 1834 the commercial hotel 'Danieli' was still something of a new venture in Venice. For centuries this building close to the Doge's palace had been known as Palazzo Dandalo. By the time of Napoleon's forcible dissolution of the Venetian republic in 1797, the owners had ceased to maintain it. In 1822 an entrepreneur from nearby Fiuli called Giuseppe Dal Niel rented the *piano nobile* (first floor) of Palazzo Dandalo. In it he accommodated paying guests. By 1824, business was good enough to convince Dal Niel that there was a market for such a venture in Venice and he bought the entire building, lavishly restoring it and converting it into a hotel, to which he gave his Venetian nickname, 'Danieli'.

As a palazzo of the nobility, the building's main entrance had been to the side on Rio del Vin for gondola access, but as a hotel it needed a door directly onto the quayside of Riva degli Schiavoni. Dal Niel remodelled this facade to create a Gothic doorway and it was on the first floor immediately above this door that George Sand and Alfred de Musset took a suite with superb views. On a clear day you could see beyond the island of San Giorgio di Maggiore to Lido.

When I stepped off the vaporetto in 1994 Hotel Danieli was immediately recognisable by its pink facade and pointed ogee windows. I crossed the Ponte del Vin over a narrow canal to reach it. The old stone bridge is much busier today than it would have been in 1834. These days Venice is almost submerged by tourists, but at the beginning of the nineteenth century it was a shadow of its former proud and prosperous self, struggling as a new Habsburg appendage, thanks to Napoleon.

Inside the hotel lobby I made my way through costumed revellers to the concierge's desk at the bottom of a great stone staircase. Originally this had stood open to the skies in the days when it was the palazzo's courtyard, but Dal Niel glassed it over. Descending this staircase has since become one of the most splendid ways to make an entrance in Venice. As I arrived it was serving that function for a huge party of wealthy Egyptian and Lebanese wedding guests. Every night they were dining – in extravagant Carnival dress – at a different palazzo.

Although Sand and de Musset were in Venice during the period preceding Lent when 'Carnevale' had been celebrated for centuries, the festival had been banned in 1797 by the Habsburgs, and the wearing of masks was outlawed on moral grounds. Carnevale was not revived in George Sand's time. In fact in its present exotic and erotic form, it is essentially a 1980s phenomenon.

By contrast Venice in the 1830s had very little to offer in terms of diversion. De Musset did manage to quickly lose a lot of Sand's money at the Casino, however – and then fall ill from a combination of nervous exhaustion and alcohol.

The manager showed me up to Room 10 where George Sand nursed her highly-strung lover for a few weeks before losing patience with him. Sand was not the kind of woman who found fulfilment tending to those who coped less well with the world than she. Five years later on Mallorca, in the winter of 1838–9, she would similarly lose patience with the morbidity of her more famous lover, Frédéric Chopin.

Sand herself always worked at a phenomenal rate, producing 43 (now mostly unread) novels in her lifetime. While in Room 10 she was working on her tenth, *André* (published 1834) and her new Italian novel *Simon* (1835). She claimed to write from eight to thirteen hours a day.

The Room 10 that I saw was decorated in shades of pale green and its floor-space was reduced in size by a bathroom and fitted wardrobes. Nevertheless it retains that wonderful view across to San Giorgio. Someone has gallantly stencilled 'Alfredo de Musset e George Sand MDCCCXXXIII–XXXIV' over the partition, but Room 10 was hardly a love nest. De Musset was not just ill, but jealous and hysterical in turns. He rightly suspected that Sand was taking solace in the company of the doctor she had called to help with her increasingly deranged lover. Dr Pietro Pagello was both young and handsome. Very soon he had cured de Musset of his vapours and cured Sand of any remaining love for her poet. De Musset accepted the situation and left for Paris on 29 March. Sand and the doctor stayed on in Venice until August when she took him to Paris, but soon decided he was dull, and abandoned him.

Today Sand's novels have fallen out of fashion and, like Vita Sackville-West, she is better known for her lifestyle than her literature. Photographs do not show a sexual siren but a rather podgy, heavy-featured middle-aged woman. Nevertheless her energy and her daring insistence on a woman's right to take lovers, as men took mistresses, clearly had an impact on those who encountered her.

Chopin claimed to be repulsed by Sand on their first meeting, but he nevertheless fell under her spell. She would eventually parody their relationship in the novel *Lucrezia Floriani* (1846), in which Chopin was the model for a sickly Eastern European prince named Karol, while Sand is Lucrezia, a middle-aged actress past her prime, who suffers for caring too much about the selfish Prince Karol.

The Danieli had many distinguished guests after George Sand, including Wagner, Dickens and Benjamin Britten, but it's unlikely that any of them loved so passionately nor grew so quickly disenchanted as George Sand and her 'Alfredo'.

PALAZZO BARBARO, VENICE – HENRY JAMES (1843–1916)

Before Hollywood decided en masse that Paris was the most romantic city in the world, wealthy Americans were besotted with Italy. This love affair continued throughout the nineteenth century. Rome and Florence were very popular among the American expat community, and so was Venice.

Of all the crumbling palaces patronised by American visitors none was such a favourite as Palazzo Barbaro on the Grand Canal near Accademia Bridge. As an enthusiast for the 'Barbaro Circle' I've often gazed over at it and thought about the writers and artists who had the good fortune to stay there.

It's a fine Gothic structure made up of two interlinked palaces. The first, on the left if you are looking at them from

the Grand Canal, was built in 1425 by Giovanni Bon, one of Venice's master stonemasons, for the Spiera family. In 1465 it was bought by Zaccaria Barbaro, who was Procurator of San Marco, the second most important office in Venice.

The palazzo on the right was built two centuries later in the Baroque style by the architect Antonio Gaspari for the Tagliapietra family, one of the 30 families allowed to sit in the Great Council. As this was only a two-storey palazzo, the Tagliapietras gave permission for Gaspari to build over it in 1694, adding a lofty ballroom for the Barbaro family. The stuccoed and gilded ballroom was decorated by Sebastiano Ricci's titillating painting 'The Rape of the Sabine Women' and frescoes by Giovanni Battista Piazzetta.

The American connection was not established until 1881 when two floors of the older palazzo were rented by Daniel Sargent Curtis, a cousin of the American portraitist John Singer Sargent. Curtis purchased his floors outright four years later, and set about restoring them with his wife Ariana. The couple soon made Palazzo Barbaro the centre of American artistic life in Venice. John Singer Sargent visited and famously painted a portrait of Daniel's daughter-in-law, Mrs Ralph Curtis, in a white ball-gown.

The painters Anders Zorn, Claude Monet and James McNeill Whistler also visited and worked at Palazzo Barbaro. Visiting writers included Robert Browning, Edith Wharton, and that lover of Europe's grand houses, Henry James.

James and Palazzo Barbaro, both of them overwrought and yet secretive, were a perfect match. James had first visited the city in 1869 as a bearded young disciple of John Ruskin. He was immediately taken with the city, but recorded that he would never get to know it from within. When in 1894 his close friend, the novelist Constance Fenimore Woolson, committed suicide in Venice by throwing herself from a palazzo casement, Venice became a darker place in James' imagination. In 1899 he noted that a Venetian palazzo's 'beautiful blighted rooms' could be the setting of a novel about the owners' fallen fortunes.

James included Venice in his travel writing, *From Venice to Strassburg* (1873) and *Italian Hours* (1909). In between, while staying as a guest of the Curtises, he finished writing his 1888 novella, *The Aspern Papers* – based on a true story that he deliberately transplanted to Venice to spare blushes – and the desk at which he worked is still in the palace today. It's a rather elaborate bureau in black lacquer with Chinese figures picked out in gold. Later James used the palazzo as a setting in his novel, *The Wings of the Dove* (1902). With his customary discretion he disguised Barbaro as Palazzo Leporelli, but it's clear that his lengthy description of the ballroom is a pen portrait of the Barbaro's – which James told everyone was the finest example of a Venetian Baroque interior.

Like many tourists, I've often photographed Palazzo Barbaro from Dorsoduro and the Accademia bridge. Until recently much of it was owned by the Curtis family and the doorbell on Fondamenta Barbaro still reads 'Curtis' in black letters.

When the Italian bicycle magnate Ivano Beggio bought the palazzo, I contacted an Italian academic who had befriended him on Facebook and managed to gain access through her. The open courtyard has the Curtis family's huge black gondola drawn up on the cobbles, and there are steep steps up to the *piano nobile*. I noticed a lot of plaster had fallen off the external walls.

Even in Henry James' time the palazzo was a shadow of its former self. When the Barbaro family died in the 1850s, much that could be sold off was, including all its Tiepolos and a collection of books that was said to be one of the best private libraries in Venice. But the *portego*, a corridor linking the drawing rooms, was broad and gracious and I could imagine James relishing the sense of calm that comes from so much space.

Nevertheless, while James was writing – and sleeping – in the Barbaro's third floor all this decayed grandeur proved inspirational. So much that could be innocent and beautiful in life is, in Henry James' novels, soured. In Venice he found an apt metaphor for that world view.

GRAND HÔTEL DES BAINS, VENICE – THOMAS MANN (1875–1955)

Thomas Mann's *Der Tod in Venedig* (*Death in Venice*) is a book shot through with sadness. Mann wrote the novella, today one of his most popular stories, after staying at the Grand Hôtel des Bains on Venice's Lido in 1911. Like Gustav von Aschenbach, the artistic hero of the book, Mann became fascinated by a beautiful young Polish boy whose family were also staying at the hotel. Mann based his hero Aschenbach on Gustav Mahler, whom he had met in Vienna and who'd recently died of a heart attack, but whereas Mahler expired at the peak of his creative powers, Aschenbach is depicted as suffering writer's block.

The boy was later identified as ten-year-old Baron Władysław Moes, whose first name was usually shortened to Władzio. Thomas Mann's wife insisted that her husband never followed Władzio round Venice as Aschenbach followed his beloved 'Tadzio'. Nevertheless many believe the book hints at suppressed homoerotic tendencies, which were confirmed twenty years after Mann's death when his diaries were published.

I can't help thinking that in the years to come the underlying sadness in the book touched both the hotel and the young boy. At the end of his life, Baron Moes recalled that summer in 1911 in an interview: 'I was considered to be a very beautiful child and women admired and kissed me when I walked along the promenade. Some of them sketched and painted me ... The writer must have been highly impressed by my unconventional clothes and he described them without missing a detail: a striped linen suit and a red bow-tie as well as my favourite blue jacket with gold buttons.'

The long 'Edwardian summer' of European peace was about to end, however. The First World War would see Thomas Mann's country in conflict with Italy and during the Second World War Germany held Władzio captive for six years. In 1945, after the cessation of hostilities, all his property was confiscated by the new Communist regime in Poland. He died in 1986 before his country managed to throw off the government that had been imposed upon it after a war that, ironically, had been started to save Poland from foreign invasion.

The Grand Hôtel des Bains had a less traumatic time in the twentieth century, but is a sorry sight if you visit it today. By a fitting coincidence it opened in 1900, the same year that Władzio was born. This was Venice's first great resort hotel, built on the spit of land known as Lido that separates the Venetian lagoon from the Adriatic. It was indeed a splendid sight, with a porticoed entrance held up by eight Corinthian columns, four floors of bedrooms, and beautifully manicured grounds. The hotel attracted wealthy Italians as well as European aristocrats seeking sunshine, and celebrities like the ballet impresario Serge Diaghilev

(who entertained his many lovers at Hôtel des Bains, and in 1929 died there).

The opening of a private airport at Nicelli on the northernmost tip of Lido (three kilometres from Hôtel des Bains) and the patronage of the charismatic poet, politician and aviator Gabriele D'Annunzio, only increased its appeal. But the Grand Hôtel des Bains was always cut off from the seaside by its garden and by the long beach road, now known as Lungomare Guglielmo Marconi. It was soon to be eclipsed by the opening of the much larger Grand Hotel Excelsior in 1908. The Excelsior had the advantage of being directly on the beach, and its lobby could be accessed by motor launches coming from Venice via a specially-dug canal. This was a twentieth-century hotel in an over-the-top Moorish style while Hôtel des Bains remained rooted in the nineteenth. All the older lady could do to compete was to create a pedestrian tunnel under Lungomare Guglielmo Marconi.

After the Second World War the gradual rediscovery of Venice itself as a destination meant that Lido faced increased competition. It was likely that only one major hotel could survive long-term.

As guest numbers dwindled, the hotel's beach and exteriors were used by Visconti in 1971 when he filmed *Death in Venice*, although its interiors were shot on a sound stage in Cinecittà in Rome. Visconti memorably emphasised the parallels with Mahler by making his Aschenbach – played by Dirk Bogarde – a composer rather than author. Hôtel des Bains was also used as a movie location in the 1996 film of *The English Patient*, but in 2010 the hotel closed for good. It was going to be converted into a luxury apartment complex called Residenze des Bains. Five years later, though, when I last looked over the fence that currently surrounds it, no work was going on and the portico was boarded up.

Der Tod in Venedig was a success for Thomas Mann, who went on to win the Nobel Prize for Literature in 1929 and the Goethe Prize in 1949. The film of it was also good for the careers of Dirk Bogarde and Visconti, and helped revive interest in Mahler's work, but 1911 proved to be a high-water mark for Baron Władysław Moes, and the hotel on Lido that welcomed in his family that summer.

GRITTI PALACE, VENICE – ERNEST HEMINGWAY (1899–1961)

Ernest Hemingway came to Venice a number of times in his adventurous 61 years. More than anyone else perhaps, this heavy-drinking American novelist exemplifies our idea of the twentieth-century writer as traveller to exotic places and lover of expensive hotels. Paris and Pamplona, Cuba and Kenya were Hemingway's destinations of choice. He also had a particular soft spot for northern Italy, where as a young man he had seen very brief service in the First World War as a field medic.

The island of Torcello and the south-east end of the Grand Canal were Hemingway's stomping grounds in Venice. He liked Harry's, a compact super-expensive cocktail bar opposite Santa Maria della Salute where both the Bellini cocktail and carpaccio were invented. Hemingway claimed to have had a hand in crafting its dry martini, which is served in a small glass without a stem and is made with ten parts gin to one part vermouth. This is an adaptation of the Montgomery (fifteen parts gin to one part dry vermouth).

Most assertions that Hemingway made about himself have to be viewed with caution, however. He was such a fabulist

that it can be difficult to separate his own exotic, wealthy and highly successful literary life from the boasts he made about it. Venice proved the location for one of the most outrageous – and embarrassing – autobiographical fictions Hemingway ever wove. Here was the setting for the 'love affair' that spawned his novella *Across the River and into the Trees*. It was begun in Italy in 1948 and revised at the Gritti Palace in 1950, the hotel getting a walk-on role in the novel.

The Gritti Palace, which stands half a kilometre west of Harry's Bar, was commissioned as a Grand Canal palazzo by the Pisani family in 1475 and later bought by Doge Andrea Gritti. Its canal facade once had vivid frescoes by Giorgione but now it presents a plain brick face, broken up only by narrow stone casements to passing vaporetti.

After decades of use as lodgings for visiting diplomats, Palazzo Pisani Gritti became in the nineteenth century an annexe to the Grand Hotel Venice next door. An upper storey to accommodate less wealthy guests was added. John and Effie Ruskin came to stay in 1849, soon after their famously disastrous honeymoon. Ruskin of course preferred the original sections of the building, praising the capitals of the Palazzo Pisani Gritti's first-floor windows as 'singularly spirited and graceful' in his *Stones of Venice*.

My wife and I also stayed at the Gritti soon after our wedding – much more pleasantly than did the Ruskins – and we went back in 2013 just as the hotel completed a major refurbishment. Those renovations included remodelling the Hemingway Suite, which had been created out of first-floor rooms 115 and 117, where it was understood the author had stayed in 1950. Of course we wanted to stay in his room – but then so did everyone else in 2013.

We did get to look around and take photos, however. Compared with many 'famous author' rooms around the world, this one is pretty authentic. Hemingway was a major celebrity in the years 1948–50 when he visited Venice, and so much relating to him was preserved. When the Gritti closed for eighteen months of refurbishment 65 years later, every item of furniture, every picture and Murano glass chandelier was labelled and stored, and its original position marked, which is why I could be fairly certain that Papa Hemingway must have sat in that unremarkable low green chair in the corner of his drawing room with its well-stocked bar, models of his motor launch The Pilar and pieces of coral. I took my turn posing in the chair, I couldn't help thinking he would have found the suite that bears his name a bit over-decorated, and more to the taste of 'Miss Mary', his hard-faced fourth wife who is pictured on the wall opposite. She and Papa are snapped standing on the terrace of the Gritti during one of her visits to the hotel. Hemingway, although not yet 50, looks prematurely grandpaternal in a tweed suit.

At the time that black and white photo was taken, both were recovering from recent injuries and infections, and Hemingway was infuriating Miss Mary with his latest infatuation. He had recently fallen for a young Venetian countess and amateur artist, Adriana Ivancich. She was only nineteen and unaware of the strength of his feelings. Frustrated, Hemingway poured his passion into the worst book he ever wrote. *Across the River and into the Trees* is a thinly-veiled fantasy in which an old American colonel, 'marked for death', is having an all-but-consummated affair with Renata, a young Venetian aristocrat. Hem began the book fuelled by crates of Amarone della Valpolicella supplied by Harry's Bar round the corner.

Rereading this slim novel in Venice I felt rather sorry for the author, physically old before his time, staggering back to the Gritti at night or waking painfully early as light from the surface of the Grand Canal played on the ceiling above his bed. Did he drag a bottle of Valpolicella and the *Herald Tribune* to the lavatory with him, as his hero Colonel Cantwell does?

When the book came out, it was a critical disaster. Worse, Hemingway made the guilty mistake of dedicating his book of Adriana fantasies to Miss Mary. No wonder she looked so tight-lipped in that photo. Ironically, the critical mauling that Hemingway received for *Across the River and into the Trees* spurred him to hit back with *The Old Man and the Sea*, which won him the Nobel Prize for Literature in 1954. I'm sure, however, that Mary Hemingway would have had something tart to say about the fact that the cover illustration of that novel was drawn by the young woman he had fallen in love with in Venice.

Unaware of their fantasy love affair, Adriana subsequently took up the Hemingways' invitation to visit the couple in Cuba. When Hemingway confessed his love, she was shocked. Moreover, her mother was appalled when *Across the River and into the Trees* was published in the States. Its insinuations might have damaged her daughter's marriage prospects. Hemingway forbade the book's publication in Italy for two years to spare her embarrassment. He might have done better not to have written it at all.

Ernest Hemingway committed suicide eleven years later in 1961, having lost the ability to write. Adriana, in the midst of a nervous breakdown, committed suicide in 1983 at the age of 53.

The Gritti Palace also has author suites dedicated to John Ruskin and W. Somerset Maugham. I just hope of the three of them that Maugham, even though he was not in the best of health at the time of his visits, had a happier time than Ruskin and Hemingway.

PIAZZA DI SPAGNA, ROME – JOHN KEATS (1795–1821)

For a writer who died almost unknown in 1821, it's remarkable that John Keats is commemorated in not just one house but two. The Regency villa that the poet occupied with Charles Brown in John Street, Hampstead is now open to the public as Keats House (standing in what is now known as Keats Grove). Here the young Londoner and trainee doctor wrote many of his best poems, including the odes 'To a Nightingale' and 'On a Grecian Urn'.

The second-floor apartment at Piazza di Spagna 26 in Rome, where Keats died at the age of 25, is also kept as a memorial to him. It's known today as the Keats–Shelley House despite the fact that Shelley never visited Keats during his three months in this house. Shelley was, however, in Italy when he heard of Keats' death and he wrote the poem 'Adonaïs' in response. In 1906 the house, also known as Casina Rossa, was purchased for the Keats Shelley Memorial Association, hence its name. Today it contains an archive of material relating to a range of British romantic poets, including Byron, Wordsworth, the Brownings, and Oscar Wilde.

The lure of the Keats–Shelley House is strong. It stands at the bottom of the picturesque Spanish Steps, known in Italian as Scalinata di Trinità dei Monti. These steps have featured in so many films – including *Roman Holiday* and *The Talented Mr Ripley* – that they've become a tourist attraction in their own right. However, in the eighteenth century when they were built, they served a purely practical function: linking the Trinità dei Monti church at the top of the Pincian Hill with the Bourbon-Spanish Embassy in Palazzo Monaldeschi below.

Photo: © Kate Tadman-Mourby

The monumental staircase – essentially a gigantic flight of Baroque garden steps – took from 1723 to 1725 to complete. The architects were Francesco de Sanctis and Alessandro Specchi. They wanted to frame the steps with two identical buildings at their base, which is why Babbington's Tea Rooms at Piazza di Spagna 23 is an almost mirror image of the Keats–Shelley House on the opposite side.

When John Keats was brought here by his friend, the English portrait painter Joseph Severn, the area around Piazza di Spagna was regarded by many Romans as Spanish territory because of the many years of ambassadorial presence. It was a somewhat bohemian area, a place where foreigners could lodge cheaply. A second-floor apartment was found here for the two English men by Dr James Clark, a Scotsman living in Rome.

Keats initially recovered something of his health in the rooms that he and Severn rented, and he was able to dictate some letters. The poet liked to listen to the sound of the water in the Fontana della Barcaccia, designed by Bernini in the piazza below, and to the footfall of people on the steps.

My wife and I visited the Spanish Steps one remarkable January day when Rome was unexpectedly embraced by snow. The city had never looked lovelier – snowfall beautifully highlighted the carved details on so many dark facades – but the population was coping very badly. There were no snow-ploughs to clear the roads, nor even any grit or salt for traction – and fashionable Italian leather soles have no grip of their own. Rome was a city slipping and sliding that Saturday morning.

We toured the centre as far as the icy Spanish Steps, though we dared not go up them. Instead we dropped into the steaming melee which was Babbington's Tea Rooms and here we drank hot chocolates that were very thick and dark, like rich bitter custard. Then we decided to see if the Keats–Shelley House was open. To our great surprise it was.

You enter – as he would have – up a flight of stone steps. At the top there's a small bookshop and ticket office and then it is two more flights, to the *salone*, a long room at one end of which Keats' landlady lived behind a curtained archway. What had been Severn's room lies at the opposite end of the salone, and Keats' bedroom is off that, making Severn's room in effect an antechamber.

Sadly, by the time Keats arrived here – November 1820 – the sunshine of Italy was in short supply and he gained virtually no benefit from his long journey south. Keats had a bed in this room and a fireplace where Severn heated up food for him, but the current bed, the painted wood panelling in the room and even the window casements are relatively new. At the time of John Keats' death, Vatican law required that everything in a room where someone died of consumption had to be burned to restrict the danger of contagion.

So since 1906 the room in which poor Keats died has been restored as well as it can be, and painted an authentic, peaceful light blue. The famous portrait by Severn of Keats on his deathbed hangs over the *letto a barca*, a style of carved boat bed that dates from the time of the poet's death.

That January morning there were a number of young women looking around the rooms of Keats and Severn, and the displays on British romantic poets in what had previously been the apartment of their landlady. The women were mostly serious and taking photos of the items rather than selfies. Some were even dipping into volumes of his poetry.

Just about every literary room I've visited has witnessed either the genesis of a book or its writing. Sadly, the Keats–Shelley House is all about the death of a young poet who was no longer writing but who had come to Rome in the hope of a cure, and if not a cure then the easing of his passage from this life. John Keats did not compose anything beyond those letters dictated to Severn during his last painful months in Rome. He died in February 1821, believing himself to have failed as a poet. And yet, more than many places I have visited, this was a room all of his own.

PENSION SIMI, FLORENCE – E.M. FORSTER (1879–1970)

If ever there was a novel where the right room seemed essential, it's E.M. Forster's *A Room with a View*, which he began in December 1901 after staying in Florence. 'She promised us south rooms with a view,' exclaims Lucy Honeychurch's cousin as the two women find themselves facing into a courtyard rather than overlooking the Arno. The fact that Mr Emerson and his son George gallantly offer up their river-view rooms puts the ladies into a very Forsterian, English middle-class spin from which Lucy does not recover until the end of the book. In the last pages of Forster's novel we find Lucy and George back in Pension Bertollini, happily married and listening to the sounds of the river from their ideal room with a view.

E.M. Forster actually stayed in a hotel on a section of Lungarno (Arno embankment) on several occasions between 1901 and 1903. In those days it was known as Pension Simi at Corso Tintori 7, and he first made its acquaintance in October 1901 while holidaying with his mother. Although the building's address is on the Corso, its front door opens on to the section of the riverbank known as Lungarno alla

Grazie. The Forsters took two rooms, one on the ground floor and one on the *piano nobile*. The latter would have been the room with the view across the river.

Forster, of independent means but not exactly wealthy and with not one but two second-class degrees from Cambridge behind him, was 22 years old. He was unsure what to do with his life, although he had already started writing. In Florence he was still battling with his first attempt at a novel. *Nottingham Lace*, the story of a young man spurning conventional thinking, was not going well and the question of bedrooms with or without views inspired Forster to abandon it and start his best-loved novel. *A Room with a View*, his second Italian novel, was finally published in 1908 and later filmed to great international acclaim in 1985.

Before arriving in Florence I did some research into Pension Simi, on which Forster had based his fictional Bertollini. It later took the name Hotel Pension Jennings-Riccioli and it is now a series of apartments. Next door at Corso Tintori 3 stands Palazzo Guasconi, a slightly smaller building which was the home of the fifteenth-century humanist writer Cristoforo Landino. Botticelli painted him around 1460 standing next to Federico Montefeltro, the great hook-nosed Duke of Urbino.

From my hotel – on the opposite side of the Arno – I made a number of enquiries about visiting Corso Tintori 7 but no one replied. The apartment block has 24 brass bells on its massive exterior, and is built in the Renaissance style around a number of inner courtyards which allow light into its back rooms. The cheaper of those 24 apartments would face inwards. My guess was that as a pension, Simi would have taken up only part of that big city block, perhaps the south-facing quarter at most, although a poster showed how it later expanded along the Lungarno when it became Jennings-

Photo: Adrian Mourby

Riccioli. Today the building contains a few businesses, a lot of private residences and the Florence campus of Connecticut's Fairfield University. It also does not see itself as a tourist attraction, which I suppose is why no one replied to my importuning. I turned up nevertheless one hot and humid afternoon to look for its view. You never knew if you might get lucky.

Several years earlier I had been in Rangoon with a reporter from the *Daily Mail* who'd suddenly said 'Let's go and see Aung San Suu Kyi'. The Lady was living under virtual house arrest at the time but my colleague, an inveterate door-stepper, thought if we turned up with some flowers and a bowl of fruit we might be let through. This is exactly what we did – and it worked. We were admitted, thanked for the flowers and even got a brief interview and a photo with The Lady herself.

This didn't seem such a good idea at the former Pension Simi. Aung San Suu Kyi had good reasons to meet the press. The owners of these apartments do not. So I looked at their view and the building itself. It is monumental, like so many of these Florentine city blocks. No. 7 is strictly symmetrical with a balconied *piano nobile* and two floors of bedrooms above that – and probably more in the roof. If you had booked a room with a view, it certainly would have been something worth insisting upon, because the windows not only overlook the Arno but beyond that Palazzo Serristori (where Joseph Bonaparte, brother of Napoleon, lived in exile till his death in 1844) and Piazzale Michelangelo (built in 1869 when Florence was, briefly, the capital of the new Kingdom of Italy). These days you can also see a beach that has been created in the river bed, which was certainly not there in E.M. Forster's time.

No one came or went while I hung around Lungarno delle

Grazie so I did not get to see whichever room with a view E.M. Forster might have coveted when he stayed here with his mother. However, I did come to realise that whereas it is a view north to the Duomo that ends the lovely Merchant Ivory film of 1985, what the English tourists in Forster's novel aspire to is the view south across the river. I also realised that Chiesa Santa Croce is just around the corner from Corso Tintori 7, a few hundred yards at most. No wonder that was where Lucy Honeychurch went on her first exploration of the city with Miss Lavinia Lavish. The fact that Miss Lavish gets them monumentally lost by turning *right* out of the pensione is not surprising. You most definitely turn left to get to Santa Croce.

So I didn't get to see E.M. Forster's 'Room of One's Own' but I certainly found the pension and the views. After all, it was the view looking out, not the room itself, that was always Forster's priority.

SOUTHERN ENGLAND

BROAD STREET, LYME REGIS, DORSET – JANE AUSTEN (1775–1817)

Jane Austen's output of novels was remarkable given her short life and that she wrote them in her spare time, allegedly hiding pages under her sewing when someone came into the drawing room. For an author who was virtually unknown in her lifetime, it is even more remarkable that today she finds her way on to university syllabuses while simultaneously supplying plots that appeal to TV and cinema audiences.

Less noteworthy – but still interesting to me – is the fact that almost all the settings for her novels are fictional. Two rare exceptions are the city of Bath and the seaside town of Lyme Regis. Both were described in some detail in her last, posthumously published novel, *Persuasion*. We know from her letters that Jane did not much like Bath, but she clearly loved Lyme, as can be discerned in some enthusiastic passages in the second half of *Persuasion*.

So when I went in search of Miss Austen I thought I'd track her down in this Dorset resort. It has been mercifully preserved from the overdevelopment that affected most British seaside towns in the Edwardian era and the sordid contraction that then blighted them at the end of the twentieth century.

From medieval times Lyme was a trading port for the export of wool and the import of wine. It was also a centre of ship-building. Because it did not possess a natural harbour, local engineers created the Cobb, a long curving stone arm jutting out into the sea, constructed out of boulders held in place by tree trunks. This impressive piece of Tudor engineering helped Lyme withstand a two-month siege during the English Civil War when it could only be resupplied by sea.

Almost continual war with France in the eighteenth century led to Lyme's decline as a seaport, but it was rescued commercially by the new fashion for sea-bathing that was given royal support by George III. From 1789 the king took annual recuperative trips to nearby Weymouth. Thomas Hollis, a local landowner, was the great pioneer of Lyme as a sea-bathing resort. Hollis bought up and redeveloped much of the semi-derelict town and created 'The Walk', a public promenade (now known as the Marine Parade). He also built the Assembly Rooms at the end of Broad Street, on the site of some abandoned shipping warehouses.

By the time Jane Austen visited Lyme Regis with her mother and father – in 1803 and 1804 – Hollis' attempts to create a resort were paying off handsomely. The Assembly Rooms, where Jane liked to dance, were perched romantically on the harbour wall with the sea breaking beneath them. During her second visit, in 1804, Jane wrote to her sister: 'The ball last night was pleasant, but not full for Thursday. My father staid [*sic*] contentedly till half-past nine (we went a little after eight), and then walked home with James and a lanthorn [lantern], though I believe the lanthorn was not lit, as the moon was up, but sometimes this lanthorn may be a great convenience to him. My mother and I staid [*sic*] about an hour later.'

By Jane's time Broad Street was busy and lined with hotels, shops and a meat market. Jane described the road's

precipitate steepness as 'almost hurrying into the water' and she praised the Walk as 'skirting round the pleasant little bay, which, in the season, is animated with bathing machines and company'.

Perversely I arrived in winter. The summer crowds had disappeared, which meant I was able to walk down Broad Street without interruption. It is indeed steep, with a little terrace built for access to No. 10, which is now the Mulberry Manor pie shop. The large blue front door next to it leads to five apartments carved out of the old house; those above the shop face the street while the others face back towards the sea. Above this door is a small plaque left by the Austen Society that reads: 'This is the most likely lodging of Jane Austen.'

The reason we believe Jane stayed here at No. 10 is that she had some correspondence with a Mr Pyne in Lyme concerning a broken jug. On a map of 1824 a cottage belonging to William Pyne Esquire is marked in this position with The Shambles (the cattle market) held immediately below it. Jane's little terrace would have looked down on the quayside Assembly Rooms, which were unfortunately demolished to make way for a car park in the second half of the twentieth century.

With the Assembly Rooms gone and many of the shopfronts sporting twenty-first-century veneers, it is hard to get a feel for the world of Jane's heroine, Anne Elliot and Wentworth, her naval captain. Broad Street is much more recognisable as the location for opening scenes in the 1981 film *The French Lieutenant's Woman*, where its two prominent hotels, the Royal Lion and the Three Cups are clearly visible, a view that would not have existed in 1803 and 1804. The current version of the Three Cups was built later and the Royal Lion was set back from Broad Street in Jane's day.

I walked along Marine Parade, following in the footsteps

of Tennyson and Hardy, who came to Lyme on their own Austen pilgrimages. These days the 'Walk' that Jane knew is a sturdy road with houses facing the beach. In her time it was intermittently washed away and only stabilised with a retaining wall in the 1820s (after her death). At this time a number of Regency-style houses were built along Marine Parade, including Harville and Benwick Cottages, renamed in recent years after Captain Wentworth's comrades. They date from around 1830 and are far too prosperous-looking for the dwellings of those impoverished Navy officers.

Finally I reached the Cobb, where a chilly wind was blowing. Satisfyingly, it looks just like you would expect it to, a huge, sloping serpentine sea wall that just cries out to be walked along. There are three sets of steps up from the harbour quayside on to the Cobb, but *Persuasion* does not specify down which set Louisa Musgrove falls. The first flight, known as the Gin Shop Steps, are very safe and sturdy. The second, known as Granny's Teeth, are challenging even if you are not wearing eighteenth-century clothing. The third sequence, a modern concrete addition, obviously would not have been there in Jane's time (and anyone who has seen the film of *The French Lieutenant's Woman* will know that a temporary fourth flight of steps was built so that Meryl Streep as Sarah Woodruff could ascend them easily without tripping over her voluminous black cloak).

It is extraordinary that a harbour wall in Dorset has played such a pivotal role in two great English novels, but on that particular day more people were talking about Jane than John Fowles. 'Are these Louisa Musgrove's Steps?' a young couple asked me as they took a selfie. Can there be any more satisfying tribute than to have a part of a town you love renamed in the popular imagination after one of your fictional characters?

THE ACORN INN, EVERSHOT, DORSET – THOMAS HARDY (1840–1928)

The Dorset village of Evershot claims a double connection with Thomas Hardy.

As a young architect, still living in his parents' home in Higher Bockhampton, Hardy trained at Rampisham, just two miles from Evershot. There is a local legend that before he gave up architecture to marry and to write full-time in 1873, Hardy designed a splendid new drawing room for the local dower house at 9 Fore Street. He also featured Evershot's one pub in three of his fictions. So when I received an invitation one November to visit 'Thomas Hardy's Historic Acorn Inn', I seized upon it.

Driving downhill into Evershot I passed a thatched house that has been renamed 'Tess Cottage'. It stands close to St Osmond's church (which coincidentally was where the poet George Crabbe, 1754–1832, had been the titular rector – although he seems not to have ever lived in Evershot). Continuing down icy West Hill from the church I saw a big black and white sign on Fore Street proclaiming Thomas Hardy's 'historic inn'. I parked and did a quick reconnoitre of the 200-person village before checking in. There was a post office-cum-village shop, a doctors' surgery, a primary school, a thriving bakery, and yet more thatched cottages. Even without the three fictional connections you'd look around and exclaim: 'This is pure Thomas Hardy!'

The Acorn Inn (renamed the Sow-and-Acorn by Hardy) features in two of his short stories, 'Interlopers at the Knap' (1884) and 'The First Countess of Wessex' (1889), as well as in a particularly painful section of *Tess of the D'Urbervilles*

(1891) where Tess breakfasts at a cottage by the church rather than entering the Sow-and-Acorn.

My room (named after a fictional Hardy village) was comfortable with a window seat, large four-poster bed, walls upholstered in hessian, an authentically sloping floor and a cast-iron fireplace that would have been working in Hardy's day. The staircase seemed unusually wide for a village inn, but then in Thomas Hardy's youth women's dresses reached ridiculous widths.

After looking at the names of the other rooms – all taken from Hardy – I went for afternoon tea at the Summer Lodge Country House Hotel, which is what the old dower house is called nowadays. There was fabric on the walls here too, though this time it was light blue and matched the drawing room sofas. There were two deep recesses either side of the fireplace – each like a little room in its own right.

I asked the sales manager if there was any paperwork proving that Hardy designed the drawing room and the master bedroom above, and he admitted he'd found none yet. So many buildings in this part of Dorset are said to be Thomas Hardy's work. My feeling is that the extension is most unlikely to be his, as the person who commissioned it was the 5th Earl of Ilchester who had never forgiven Hardy for using an Ilchester family scandal as the basis for 'The First Countess of Wessex'. In this tale of an aristocratic elopement, the local squire's factotum Tupcombe seats himself 'in the chimney-corner of the Sow-and-Acorn' in Evershead (Hardy's name for Evershot) to learn news of the recently-eloped Betty.

Even if Hardy had drawn up the plans, trying to find the novelist who wrote *Far from the Madding Crowd*, *Tess of the D'Urbervilles* and *Jude the Obscure* in a room that he designed is a bit like trying to recognise Winston Churchill's authorial skills in the brick walls he built at Chartwell. It's a literary footnote, not an insight.

I'm all for hotels, shops and restaurants claiming some kind of literary pedigree. Compared with France and Italy, Britain names very few places after creative artists, but there wasn't much sense of Hardy yet. I don't know what I was looking for. I'd studied Hardy's novels in university and even at the time thought them self-indulgently pessimistic. *Tess of the D'Urbervilles* is almost sadistic in the way that Thomas Hardy makes sure that anything that can go wrong for his heroine does. At the end of that walk through Evershead/ Evershot, Tess hides her walking boots and changes into dainty shoes so she may appear well-dressed before her in-laws. Of course they find her boots hidden behind a tree and appropriate them for The Poor. Tess's nerve fails her before she can introduce herself, and she trudges home with wet feet and nothing accomplished.

So I made my way back up bitterly cold Fore Street to the Acorn Inn which the fictional Tess had once shunned and propped myself up by the fireplace until it was time for dinner. After the landlord had served me a restorative whisky it seemed much easier to imagine the young Thomas Hardy calling in here on a similarly cold day, his mind full of fictional characters when he should have been thinking about architecture. Why else would he have remembered this seat 'in the chimney-corner of the Sow-and-Acorn' and mentioned the pub in three of his stories?

I still think he's a major pessimist though.

LITTLE EASTON, ESSEX – H.G. WELLS (1866–1946)

H.G. Wells, the prolific English novelist and bon-viveur, was already famous when he rented an eighteenth-century vicarage on the estate of his friend Daisy, Countess of Warwick, at Little Easton. The couple were an odd match. Wells in 1910 was aged 44, a socialist who had worked his way up from the shop-keeping class to great success and wealth via a series of best-selling novels. The Countess, aged 49, was a profligate aristocrat who had been castigated in the London press for her extravagant parties in the 1890s. After losing a lot of money – and being dropped by her royal lover (the future King Edward VII) for several women younger than herself – Daisy became a socialist and hosted Trades Union events at her father's estate, Easton Lodge, to which she had retired.

When Wells became her tenant in 1910, he was unhappily married for the second time and conducting affairs with a sequence of women (in 1912 he would bed the novelist Rebecca West, 27 years his junior, and who would eventually bear his third son). Wells, who had bought a London home in Regent's Park, took to country life with his usual gusto and celebrated his time at the old vicarage in Little Easton Glebe in a largely-forgotten novel, *Mr Britling Sees It Through*.

The book was published in 1916 and had a huge impact around the world, although these days it has been eclipsed by Wells' science fiction stories (*The War of the Worlds*, *The Invisible Man* and *The Time Machine*), and perhaps also by his novels of lower-middle-class ennui like *The History of Mr Polly* and *Kipps*.

Photo: Adrian Mourby

Mr Britling Sees It Through was a wartime bestseller. After reading it, Maxim Gorky wrote to Wells: '[It is] the finest, most courageous, truthful, and humane book written in Europe in the course of this accursed war ... at a time of universal barbarism and cruelty, your book is an important and truly humane work.' Gorky and Wells were not just fellow socialists and mutual admirers. In due course they would share the same mistress – the Soviet spy, Moura Budberg.

Mr Britling Sees It Through is hardly a *roman à clef*. No key is needed to work out who is who in this novel. Britling, a short, successful, sociable, easy-going novelist living in the Essex countryside – and embarking on his eighth extramarital affair – is clearly Wells. Edith, the neglected second wife of Mr Britling, is clearly Jane, Wells' second wife who had long ago given her permission for him to pursue other women.

The book is divided into three parts. Book the First is set during the summer before the outbreak of the First World War when an American, Mr Direck, visits Britling and his son Hugh, and discusses politics with the family's German tutor, Herr Heinrich. Book the Second covers the first year of the war when Hugh Britling is killed at the front, and in Book the Third Mr Britling learns that Herr Heinrich has also been killed in the war and writes a long, compassionate letter to Heinrich's parents in Germany.

I recently drove to Easton Lodge on a wet summer's morning and found, to my disappointment and surprise, that Daisy Warwick's Victorian mansion had been demolished in the 1950s. After the Second World War her younger son, Maynard Greville, had been unable to afford the substantial repairs it required. As a keen lover of trees he then planted an arboretum over the site of the demolition.

On that damp morning, making my way through a small copse, I discovered the remains of Daisy's gardens, opened to the public by volunteers who market them as 'The Forgotten Gardens of Easton Lodge'. I found the volunteers picnicking underneath a cedar tree, now over a hundred years old, that they told me had been planted by the future Edward VII on one of his amorous visits to Daisy.

The vicarage garden where Wells organised games of hockey (compulsory for all his guests) is separated from the arboretum by a field on which the Countess used to hold the annual county fair – an event that crops up in *Mr Britling*. To get there by road, however, I had to drive round a quarter of a mile of country lanes.

After renting for a few years, Wells bought the vicarage from the Countess and renamed it Glebe Lodge. Here I met Vincent Thompson, former High Sherriff of Essex who has owned the novelist's country retreat for the last twenty years. I was certainly not the first literary pilgrim to turn up on his doorstep and after coffee, Vincent generously showed me around. From the outside, the house is substantially the same as the Georgian brick pile where Wells held rural court and wrote *Mr Britling*.

Inside, Vincent and his wife have knocked together the old scullery and adjoining servant's parlour to make a modern eat-in kitchen, but otherwise the room layout is as Wells arranged it. I was shown the dining room (painted a deep green) which Wells had extended with semi-circular windows. He decorated this unusual room with mirrors and ornate plasterwork. I also sat in his drawing room, which he extended with even bigger windows. Here he used to keep his books and listen to his wife or guests playing the piano. I also saw Wells' bath in an en-suite off the bedroom where he sometimes wrote. It was jammed in under the window and tiny. Even a man of Wells' fabled shortness would have been unable to lie down in the water. Vincent's daughter, who sleeps in the bedroom, has long campaigned to have this piece of our literary heritage replaced.

Outside we looked at the last of the seven cedars on the lawn that were truly gracious in Wells' day. We couldn't see his actual writing shed because it was demolished long ago, but Vincent showed me the corrugated iron barn that now stands where Wells produced the book that earned him a small fortune. Wells said that he felt bad about the fact that *Mr Britling*, a book written about the sadness occasioned by the First World War, made him £20,000 just for the American rights. Of course he coped with those feelings. Writers are notoriously adept at living with guilt.

Having read *Mr Britling Sees It Through*, it was easy to pace the book out at Glebe Lodge. Here was the rose garden that Mrs Britling showed to Mr Direck. Here the arbour where Miss Corner sat reading as she captured Mr Direck's heart … It's a rare treat to visit somewhere that so closely resembles the novel it inspired, though you are left wondering if Wells made any of it up at all.

SISSINGHURST CASTLE, KENT – VITA SACKVILLE-WEST (1892–1962)

The semi-moated Tudor manor house at Sissinghurst had a chequered life before being bought by Harold Nicolson and Vita Sackville-West in 1930. Four hundred years previously it was something of a ruin when the Baker family, courtiers to Henry VIII, took it over and added a new brick gatehouse and 700-acre deer park. By August 1573 it was considered opulent enough to host Queen Elizabeth I and her voracious retinue for three nights.

In the eighteenth century, however, Sissinghurst Castle

served as a prison camp for more than 3,000 French prisoners of war from the Seven Years' War (1754–63) who during their captivity pretty much trashed the place. It later became a workhouse and then a home for farm labourers.

When Vita and Harold found Sissinghurst in 1930 it was derelict again, but the diplomat-scholar and his literary wife needed a rural home where they could raise their sons. Vita, having been brought up at Knole, seat of her father, the 3rd Baron Sackville, acutely felt the lack of a castle to call her own. (The barony – and Knole itself – had bypassed her and gone to a male cousin.)

'I fell in love; love at first sight,' wrote Vita. 'I saw what might be made of it. It was Sleeping Beauty's castle.' Harold worried that restoring it would absorb all their money, but he wrote back to her: 'It is in a part of Kent we like ... I could make a lake. The boys could ride.'

And so it was here in the brick Tudor tower that Vita wrote nine of her seventeen novels, many of her books of travel and biography, and much of her poetry. She also raised two sons at Sissinghurst and worked on the garden with Harold. Both husband and wife were bisexual and although devoted to each other, enjoyed affairs outside their marriage. It is ironic, given her prodigious literary output, that Vita is better known now as a gardener, as the wife of Harold Nicolson, the mother of writers Benedict and Nigel Nicolson, and the lover of Virginia Woolf. Her fiction, written with a 'pen of brass' according to Mrs Woolf, has not stood the test of time.

I drove to Sissinghurst after visiting H.G. Wells' rural retreat in Essex. The sun had come out and the car park was full of day-trippers who were busy buying plants to take home – a souvenir of Sissinghurst – for their own gardens. I knew a bit about the layout of the place from having watched the

BBC drama, *Portrait of a Marriage,* and so went immediately to the Big Room, which sits in the corner of what resembles an open-sided Oxbridge quadrangle. When Vita and Harold arrived, this had been stables, but they panelled it and filled it with books and used the room for grand dinner parties. (In 1952 the Queen Mother came to dine.) It contains over 8,000 volumes, making it the third-biggest library belonging to the National Trust. The NT custodian explained that because Vita and Harold knew everyone who was someone, they had author-signed copies of most of the major works of the 1920s and 30s. In other books, they would often write cryptic messages to each other.

Across the lawn stands the great tower in which Vita had her Writing Room. It is accessed via an internal spiral staircase. Nigel Nicolson recalled rarely being allowed into his mother's workroom on the first floor. Today you can only see into it through a metal grille. On the desk are photos of Harold, and of Virginia Woolf, who was ten years older than Vita and something of a literary role model for her. Their affair, which lasted from 1925 till 1928, was long over when the Nicolsons moved to Sissinghurst.

The bookshelves of the room are exactly as they were left after Vita's death in 1962. There are dictionaries, books on gardening and psychology, copies of Shakespeare, Kipling and Woolf as well as all Harold's publications. To my surprise I noticed that Vita's own books were squeezed in on the bottom shelf and easy to miss.

Above the fireplace is a range of turquoise pottery and glass that Vita collected when Harold was working as a diplomat in Tehran. The room is low-lit and feels like a comfortable retreat from the world. Further up the tower there is an old printing press which was a moving-in present from Virginia and Leonard Woolf, whose Hogarth Press published many of Vita's books in the 20s and 30s. Vita was one of their bestselling authors. Continuing up to the very top of the Tudor tower, I saw where Civil Defence spotter teams used to give warning of enemy planes during the Second World War. Sissinghurst stood in 'Bomb Alley', a route through Kent that the Luftwaffe took nightly when attacking London.

Sissinghurst is now run by the National Trust and still looks as extraordinary as the woman who bought and restored it. It feels like it would be difficult to live here and *not* be a writer. Vita's tower is exactly what we imagine an author's retreat to be, unlike Virginia Woolf's spartan writing shed at Monk's House in Sussex. I wouldn't go so far as to say that Vita played at being a writer because she could write well, but, unlike Mrs Woolf, she conspicuously enjoyed the trappings of being a writer too. Her clothes, her decor, her choice of a ruined castle as her home all played up to the romantic ideal. Richard Wagner was a very similar figure, concerned with the external appearance of an *artiste* as much as the music within him.

Nigel Nicolson's gazebo where he wrote the memoir *Portrait of a Marriage* is open to the public and overlooks the remains of Sissinghurst's moat. Harold Nicolson's study in South Cottage (where he and Vita actually lived) has recently been opened up too. Both Nigel and Benedict's daughters have also written books about Sissinghurst and the remarkable people who lived and wrote here. This is not just a home, it's the focal point of a dynasty of compulsive autobiographers.

NORTHERN ENGLAND
&
NORTH WALES

DOVE COTTAGE, GRASMERE, CUMBRIA –
WILLIAM WORDSWORTH (1770–1850)

Dove Cottage was home to two distinguished writers in succession. In 1799 William Wordsworth and his sister Dorothy rented it and subsequently filled its few rooms with friends, a dog donated by Sir Walter Scott, and so many children (by William's wife Mary) that he moved the whole household out to bigger premises in 1808. At that point Thomas De Quincey, who had loved the cottage as a visitor and Wordsworth acolyte, moved in with his own wife, family and dog. There's not much of Quincey in the cottage today. A portrait now stands above the mantel in what was Dorothy Wordsworth's bedroom, with some poppy stems on the mantelpiece in a tribute to his famous opium 'eating', and there's a large circular scorch mark on the landing where Margaret De Quincey put down a bucket of hot coals to tell her children to stop squabbling. But the rest of this cottage, set back from the main road to Keswick, is essentially a shrine to William Wordsworth.

Wordsworth was a revolutionary poet who brought the subject matter of poetry back to human beings but ironically he was loved more as a writer than a person. Byron and Keats in particular admired his poetic achievements, while complaining that the older man was too full of himself.

I've always felt that Wordsworth is one of those writers whose influence has been so completely absorbed since his death that it's difficult to see now why he was considered so important. (maybe D.H. Lawrence is another.) These days the eminent Sage of Grasmere is the 'Daffodils' man, the 'Lucy' poet, and the rhymer who thought that earth had nothing more fair to show than the view from Westminster Bridge. Poor Wordsworth, it was his collaborator in *Lyrical Ballads* – and frequent house-guest – the laudanum-addicted Samuel Taylor Coleridge, who wrote *The Rime of the Ancient Mariner*, a long poem that is still read with enthusiasm today (unlike William's work). Indeed, when I visited the Wordsworth Museum Shop at Dove Cottage, Grasmere I saw that CDs of Ian McKellen reading *The Ancient Mariner* were selling well, while recordings of Wordsworth's magnum opus, *The Prelude*, were largely ignored.

After Coleridge stayed with the Wordsworths in 1810, William badmouthed him to a mutual friend, Basil Montagu, warning him of Coleridge's noisy, opium-induced nightmares. Unfortunately Montagu passed on his exact words: 'Wordsworth has commissioned me to tell you that he has no hope of you, that you have been a *rotten drunkard* and *rotted out your entrails* by intemperance, and have been an absolute nuisance in his family.' No wonder their friendship soured. I also feel it was rather mean of Wordsworth to take on the job of British Poet Laureate in 1843, collect his stipend for seven years but never come up with a single verse.

I suppose it's naive of us to expect great artists to be nice people. Nice has nothing to do with creativity. Even so, Wordsworth is probably the last literary great I'd invite to a dinner party. According to many accounts, he would dominate the conversation and talk entirely about himself.

Photo: ingawh

At least Byron would have made everyone laugh, albeit while trying to seduce my wife.

Bearing Wordsworth's temperament in mind, I wasn't best disposed towards him when parking opposite the Daffodils Hotel in Grasmere. I went first to look at St Oswald's church across the River Rydal, where the Wordsworth family tombstones are located. They are lined up in the churchyard overlooking the new 'Daffodil Garden' where you can buy Wordsworth Daffodil Bulbs to take home with you. Nearby a pink-painted shop selling canvas bags invited customers to 'Feel Free to Wander Lonely, *or as a Crowd*', and I found that the dining room at the Wordsworth Hotel is called 'The Prelude'. As a result of all this commercial exploitation, by the time I got to Dove Cottage I was beginning to feel quite sorry for poor over-marketed 'Turdsworth', as Byron referred to him.

Up until 1793 the cottage had been a public house known as the Dove and Olive Branch. When Wordsworth and his sister rented it, the downstairs floors were flagstones (typical of an English country inn where ale needed to be regularly mopped up). The whole place, its wood panelling and casements, its rickety staircase and cuckoo clock, has been well preserved thanks to the Wordsworth Trust. In 1890 they bought Dove Cottage to create a museum. The museum itself is now housed in a separate modern building and the cottage is kept as an approximation of Wordsworth's home (1799–1808).

The best room in the cottage is undoubtedly Wordsworth's study on the first floor, which would have originally had views of Grasmere (but some tall late nineteenth-century houses put paid to that). Wordsworth's chair – called a 'cavalier' because you could sit in it without removing your sword – is on display in the middle of the room. Here he would rest a pad of paper on its wide arms to write. Having taken many examinations in his university career, Wordsworth considered the desk 'an instrument of torture'. A glass cabinet nearby displays his ice skates (Wordsworth claimed he was such a good skater he could inscribe his name in the ice) and his suitcase is open on a table top. The case is tiny, but the poet believed you only needed a nightshirt, a change of shirt and a notebook when travelling. You can see that he had lettered his name into the lid. Unfortunately Wordsworth started off with characters too big so that by the time he was squeezing what remained of his name into the right-hand edge, he was reduced to 'William Wordswort'. So much for inscribing his name on a lake, I thought.

Here in this room the poet wrote – among many other pieces – the Lucy poems, 'The Ruined Cottage', 'Daffodils' (aka 'I Wandered Lonely as a Cloud'), the ode 'Intimations of Immortality, Composed upon Westminster Bridge' and the sonnet 'The World is too much with Us', one of his attacks on an increasingly industrialised society beyond the Lake District. He also worked on early drafts of *The Prelude*, a poetic autobiography that eventually ran to fourteen volumes.

The open-sided chair suggests a writer of energy who would need to get up frequently and pace while writing (Wordsworth was a passionate walker), while the skates remind me of Wordsworth's vanity. As for that suitcase: the inscription speaks of vanity *and* fallibility. The fact that Wordsworth would also leave this room only to go downstairs and complain to his sister, wife and sister-in-law that they needed to keep the children quiet also fails to endear Wordsworth to me.

I came away feeling that Dove Cottage definitely provides an insight into William Wordsworth, man and poet. I can't say I liked him any more as I left, but I did feel more connected with the man and his poetry by seeing where he wrote so much of it.

As I left, however, I'm afraid I bought *The Ancient Mariner* CD, not a recording of *The Prelude*.

THE PARSONAGE, HAWORTH, WEST YORKSHIRE – CHARLOTTE BRONTË (1816–55)

Some places where great literature was written can disappoint because they seem so unrelated to what went on in the author's head at the time. Occasionally the place has changed radically; sometimes the writer was occupying an inner landscape so personal and absorbing that he or she ignored the material world in which the writing was taking place. But then there's Haworth.

The parsonage at Haworth is to Brontë fans what Bayreuth is to Wagner's acolytes. Here is a landscape where you can believe the art was created. More exciting than anything that happened in Bayreuth, however, here is the landscape that *literally* inspired the writing.

Haworth sits on a ridge above the Bridgehouse Beck, a stream that has carved out a steep ravine in the West Yorkshire moors. In 1778 a new, plain Georgian-style parsonage was built at the top of the village, just above the church of St Michael and All Angels. In 1820 the new incumbent Patrick Brontë arrived with his wife and six children to take up the perpetual curacy.

The three youngest girls, who would go on to be Britain's first family of literary geniuses, were Charlotte (aged four),

Emily (aged two) and Anne (newly-born). There was also a brother, Branwell (then aged three) who would drink himself to death by the age of 31, and two older sisters who would die at a cheap boarding school five years after the move to Haworth. Their deaths helped inspire the early chapters of Charlotte's novel, *Jane Eyre.*

Haworth in the 1830s and 40s was a place where a lot of people died before their time. Mrs Brontë succumbed eighteen months after the family arrived. Emily died here, soon after Branwell, at the age of 29, never having realised what a success *Wuthering Heights* was becoming, and Charlotte died here too at the age of 39, having experienced success as a novelist and happiness as a wife. She was the only Brontë child to marry, and had she lived a few months longer, she would have given birth to her first baby. Anne alone of the writing triumvirate did not die in Haworth parsonage, but she would have if she'd been well enough to travel back from Scarborough where consumption did for her in 1849, also at the age of only 29.

Lest we think that the Brontës were an especially unfortunate family, it's worth remembering that Haworth was a particularly toxic place in which to live. Today it seems a rural idyll but in the early decades of the nineteenth century, rapid industrialisation had made Haworth the most polluted place in England outside the slums of London's East End. When the Brontë girls were growing up, the average life expectancy in Haworth was just 19.6 years. There were no drains in the village and human and animal effluent ran down the sides of Main Street. The village drinking water was polluted by rotting flesh from an overcrowded graveyard where Reverend Brontë worked overtime interring his parishioners.

All these grim statistics I read before visiting Haworth. Driving past signs for Brontë Country, Brontë Estate Agents

Photo: ianpudsey

and Brontë Autos, two thoughts gnawed at me: all that cramming in of people to fuel Yorkshire's industrialisation meant that the Brontë girls did not live in the wild countryside described in *Wuthering Heights* and *Jane Eyre* – and surely, tragic though their lives seem to us today, they enjoyed relatively long lives compared to most of their contemporaries in festering Haworth.

I parked at the top of a winding forested track. If you leave your car up here on Weaver's Hill and pay your £4 for the day, you walk down a picturesque footpath to the church, past pastures and chicken-runs belonging to villagers.

Coming upon the grim dark tower of the church (a late nineteenth-century construction on the site of Patrick Brontë's St Michael and All Angels) you can take a shortcut through to the parsonage or skirt the church entirely and end up in the village, which today is far cleaner than it was in the time of the Brontës. Here the apothecary's shop where Branwell bought his opium and the pub where he drank himself to death both proclaim their unfortunate Brontë connection.

I walked up the hill to the famous parsonage, which is usually photographed to exclude the lofty Victorian extension that Mr Brontë's successor, Reverend Wade, added in the 1870s. The rest of the building looks like a brighter, less gloomy and more loved version of the parsonage that we all know from the early ambrotype (a photographic print fixed on glass) from the 1850s.

Entering the parsonage, Mr Brontë's study is on the right of the hall and the family dining room, where the three daughters would walk round the table discussing their writing, is on the left. A custodian told me it's the original table which was sold off and bought back at great expense. A lot of money and research has gone into restoring the parsonage's walls and carpets to their original vivid colours, and even if the curtains in the dining room are not the originals, they exactly match the description Charlotte gave when ordering them.

As the only surviving child – and a successful writer now with money of her own to spend – Charlotte had the dining room enlarged in the 1850s. She did the same with the bedroom above which became hers on marrying her father's curate, Reverend Bell.

This enlargement of the marital bedroom was done at the expense of Emily's former bedroom over the front door. Emily was now dead and obviously had no need of it, but reducing the room meant one wall had to be demolished, and the drawings on it by the Brontë children were lost.

The wall opposite is covered with very faint sketches that the four Brontës drew when this was what servants called the Children's Study. This is the one room where the precocious siblings were undisturbed. Here the three Brontë girls acted out the plays they wrote, and dreamed up fantasy kingdoms – Angria, Gondal, Angora, Exina and Alcona – and wrote their miniature books. The drawings we can see today – heroes and heroines and attempts at self-portraits – are a direct connection with the world of the imagination that they created to escape from the unpleasantness of daily life in Haworth.

I stood entranced. So often these literary pilgrimages require an exercise of the imagination but this room is absolutely where it all began, a direct connection with the wellspring that produced three literary geniuses.

LINDETH HOWE, WINDERMERE, CUMBRIA – BEATRIX POTTER (1866–1943)

The Lake District had a huge impact on Helen Beatrix Potter, her writing and illustrations. Living in London as the eldest child of a wealthy lawyer, Beatrix was educated by governesses and grew up with few friends. The long summer holidays were spent with her family in Scotland until 1882, when they took a faux chateau on Windermere called Wray Castle. Thereafter the Potters rented for two or three months every year, settling in the end on Lindeth Howe as their holiday home of choice.

This large Victorian house had been built in 1879 and originally stood on its own in 28 acres of grounds with views over the lake. It was constructed of local slate and designed in that large-roofed, mock Tudor style that was fashionable at the end of the nineteenth century. By 1905, aged nearly 40, Beatrix was earning enough to buy her own Lake District home at Hill Top, Sawrey, on the other side of Windermere, but she was still required to spend time with her parents in Lindeth Howe, right up until her father's death in 1914.

We know from letters which she sent to her publishers, Frederick Warne & Company, that the first images of Pigling Bland, Kitty-in-Boots and the squirrel Timmy Tiptoes were sketched at Lindeth Howe. In 1911 Beatrix wrote from Lindeth that she had compressed the words in Timmy Tiptoes to fit the page, 'but it seems unavoidable to have a good deal of *nuts*'.

Beatrix's first book was published by Warne in 1902. Later the runaway success of her work meant that she was also able to buy Castle Cottage, near Hill Top, where in 1913 she moved to live with her new husband, a shy local solicitor called William Heelis.

Today it seems extraordinary that a successful writer in her 40s was expected to return to London with her family at the end of every Lake District summer holiday. And that during those vacations she was also required to commute across Windermere from Hill Top or Castle Cottage whenever her parents wanted her. Not entirely approving of Beatrix's retreat at Sawrey, the family rarely sent a car to meet her off the ferry. She may have had a room of her own on one side of the lake, but she was expected to spend a lot of time on the other.

In July 1914 Beatrix wrote to Warne from Lindeth Howe, clearly frazzled about the delay in finishing *Kitty-in-Boots*: 'We have been here three weeks already and it means nothing but going backwards and forwards. I have tried to get on with the book.'

That year Beatrix's father died. The following year Lindeth Howe came on the market and Beatrix, now a wealthy woman, bought it so her mother could remain in the Lake District nearby – but not too near. By this time Beatrix and her husband were enthusiastically breeding sheep at Castle Cottage and she'd almost stopped writing and illustrating.

Mrs Heelis, as Beatrix now styled herself, was an astute farmer but also concerned by the government's plans after the First World War to turn the Lake District into one huge conifer plantation. Her eyesight might have no longer been up to those perfectly crafted illustrations, but she had a clear vision of what she wanted to do next: buy up land to thwart the government. By the time of her death in 1941 she was able to bequeath the National Trust 4,000 acres of land, sixteen farms, plus numerous cottages and herds of cattle and sheep. Her gift made it possible for fell farming

Photo: Adrian Mourby

to continue in the Lake District rather than be driven out by forestry.

I had previously visited Hill Top, like so much of Beatrix's land now a National Trust property, but finding that Lindeth Howe was now a hotel, I decided to stay in the parental holiday home. Here in 2009 a 'Potter Room' was created out of the large south-west bedroom where Helen Potter, Beatrix's mother, slept in her widowhood.

The house lies up a hill from the Windermere ferry. It looks very like the photos taken by Beatrix's father – a keen amateur artist in his own right – but it has subtly doubled in size since his day and ten new houses have been built in the grounds, each one reducing the wide open space around the original. As the trees have grown up, the Lakeland view has all but disappeared too. Only when the trees lose their leaves in winter do you see Windermere from the lawns these days.

Inside, Lindeth Howe has the feel of a house that is moonlighting as a hotel. There is no reception and in the drawing room there are photos of Beatrix visiting Lindeth as an older woman. While I sat there waiting for my room to be ready, I watched a short film drama that the hotel has recently produced, showing Beatrix travelling from Hill Top to Lindeth Howe on foot, ferry and family car. The author is played by a local actress who specialises in reading her work. I was beginning to realise that this part of the world really values her, not so much as a famous writer but as a cherished local. This impression was further enforced by a trip I took later that day with Mountain Goat tours, which visited all the Beatrix sights including Hill Top and Wray Castle. My guide, a retired local police officer, was eloquent about Potter's work preserving the Lake District. That afternoon we saw various landscapes that found their way into the illustrations for Beatrix's books – there are no generic lanes or fences in her work – and it was nice to think that she returned the compliment, protecting the landscape that so inspired her.

At the end of the day I sat in the window of the 'Potter Room' at Lindeth Howe reading *The Tale of Timmy Tiptoes* while Japanese tourists took turns photographing each other on the garden's wooden swing seat below. Comfortable as the room was, I felt no particular connection with Beatrix or her forbidding mother in it, but the view, remarkably unspoiled by the hundred years since Beatrix bought this house, did feel like *her* view. I think that's the kind of memorial she would have wanted.

ASPINALL PLACE, MYTHOLMROYD, WEST YORKSHIRE – TED HUGHES (1930–98)

Given that being born is usually the least of a writer's achievements, I tend to avoid visiting birthplaces of famous authors but when *The Independent* invited me to be the first guest to stay in Ted Hughes' family home a few years ago, it was too tempting to resist. The birthplace of our former Poet Laureate in Mytholmroyd had just been opened as a holiday cottage. My mind boggled. Hughes was a writer of towering stature but his world – all black crows, rain and darkness – was not one you'd immediately think of vacationing in.

My drive was across Yorkshire moorland to the old cotton town of Mytholmroyd (pronounced MY-thom-roid) which nestles in a narrow industrial valley. I actually overshot and had to reverse by a genuine clog factory before finding somewhere to park in Aspinall Place.

What lay behind the lilac half-glazed door of No. 1? Would

Photo: Mark Anderson

this be a painstaking recreation of the kind of house lived in by a joiner, his wife and three children in the 1930s? I really didn't fancy pulling up a tin bath in front of the fire that evening. What I found was very like a National Trust holiday cottage. A leather sofa and armchair sat on a neutral Berber twist carpet, facing a flame-effect fireplace that was more 1930s Mayfair than Calderdale clog factory.

Only the leafed dining table and chairs were recognisably of the period. A few sepia photos were dotted around, including one on the mantel of Ted in 1938 wearing a V-neck school sweater, possibly the last time he ever smiled for a camera.

The whole place nodded in the direction of the interwar period without creating a museum. It's a holiday cottage which would like to be used by writers and, if you want it, the Birthplace Trust curator is happy to talk about Hughes. There is no shortage of local people nearby who will tell you about Ted (or even 'Teddy' as I heard him called).

There was a new kitchen and, to my relief, the bedroom of Ted's sister Olwen at the top of the steep stairs is now a modern bathroom. So no tin bath in front of a coal fire. The main bedroom where Ted was born contains a Victorian brass reproduction bed. There was also one of those awful veneered 1930s dressing tables with tall bevelled mirrors like the one that my mother inherited from her own mother. As a child I loved to angle the three mirrors carefully to create a triptych of reflections.

This conversion had probably got the tone about right, given the nearly impossible brief to refurbish an uninspiring terraced house as a desirable holiday-cottage-cum-shrine-cum-writers'-retreat. Downstairs I cleared some of the family photos off the parlour table and powered up my laptop. Sylvia Plath, who stayed here with Ted en route to Haworth, once recorded: 'I wonder if, shut in a room, I could write for a year.' All I had to do, relieved of the pressures of domestic life and friends, was to write, like her, one day at a time. It was odd to think of Sylvia and Ted off on their Brontë pilgrimage. With Haworth only ten miles away, this remote, post-industrial landscape has the most improbably grand literary connections.

That evening I'd been invited to dine with members of the Elmet Trust, who strive to keep the local connection with Ted Hughes going through ventures like 1 Aspinall Place. They'd chosen the name Elmet because, in his later years, Ted insisted that Calderdale was part of Elmet, the last Celtic kingdom in England. I walked with the secretary of the Trust down to the church hall where dinner was being held. As we passed over the Rochdale Canal, she pointed out where young Teddy and his friends used to throw stones to smash the windows of an empty factory, an act he later commemorated in the poem 'Under the World's Wild Rims'.

The dinner was a jolly occasion although our speaker made the point that Ted would never have given an after-dinner speech. He would have seen it as a frivolous waste of literary energy. While more than one member of the Trust attributed Ted's distinctive literary voice to 'Pennine gloom', they spoke of him with great fondness. For his part, the poet kept his connection with this industrial scar in the Yorkshire moors, returning often.

After an uneventful night in the room where Ted was born, I wandered round the village in morning drizzle. I got as far as Sutcliffe Farrar, a company that still produces men's trousers in Mytholmroyd. Ted's mother, Edith Farrar, was a seamstress and a relation of the owner. Evidently the modern en-suite shower off my bedroom used to be her workroom. As there was no Wi-fi in Ted's birthplace I looked for the Dusty Miller pub where the connection was said to be good, but it wasn't lunchtime yet and its doors were bolted. By now it was raining heavily so I picked up a takeaway lunch from the tiny local Sainsbury's and marched back against the brewing storm. Rain was overflowing the gutters and a lorry sent a spray of grey water over me and my little orange bag of groceries.

That afternoon, however, the weather improved and I hiked up to The Heights, a road that runs atop the surrounding hills, with one of Ted's schoolfriends. Ever since his retirement from Sutcliffe Farrar, he'd devoted himself to tracking down local references in Ted Hughes' complete oeuvre. 'There are 27 poems set in Mytholmroyd alone,' he explained as we walked up along Zion Place, 'all of them on this side of the river.' I looked at his maps that showed where the Hughes brothers used to camp, where Ted shot his first rat in a pig oile (pigsty) and where the Bessie House (a sweet shop) once stood.

The sun came out at last and I began to understand why this landscape inspired so much of Hughes' writing. As we descended from The Heights, my host pointed to a kestrel that had paused in flight, feathers fluttering above the landscape. 'That's Ted, watching over us,' he said. 'I hoped he'd be here.'

PORTMEIRION, GWYNEDD, NORTH WALES – NOËL COWARD (1899–1973)

There can be very few literary travels as successful as the train journey that Noël Coward took to North Wales in May

1941. Coward had just returned from the United States and was sure that he could help the British war effort by giving people something to laugh at. 'A light comedy had been rattling at the door of my mind,' he later claimed. In the company of his long-term friend and collaborator, actress Joyce Carey, Coward left London, which was still enduring its nightly Blitz at the hands of the Luftwaffe, and travelled north-west to Portmeirion.

The architectural fantasy village of Portmeirion had been begun in 1925 by a Welsh architect called Clough Williams-Ellis. He dubbed it, among other things, 'a home for fallen buildings'. Sir Clough did not like the modernism, functionalism and brutalism of contemporary architecture and had begun salvaging bits of old buildings he came across. He had also bought a valley along the Dwyryd estuary which he named Portmeirion. Here he reassembled them. A friend of Clough's, the sculptor Jonah Jones, described the village before the Second World War as 'a delightful hotchpotch of sometimes disparate structures, Bavarian vernacular, Cornish weather-board, Jacobean, Regency, Strawberry Hill Gothic ...'

At its centre, and nearest the estuary, stood an old hotel that Clough had restored, although from very early on guests were encouraged to stay in the eccentric cottages that he was creating on the estate. From the beginning of their joint enterprise Amabel, Clough's wife, had invited writers and artists to come to their new 'village'. One building, 'The Chantry', was built in 1937 specifically so that Augustus John might use it as a studio, but sadly the free-spirited painter never turned up.

By the time Noël Coward took up Amabel's invitation in 1941, work had temporarily ceased on the resort, but the main buildings that can be seen today were in place. He and Joyce Carey took a suite each in a building called 'The

Fountain'. Joyce described Portmeirion as 'the perfect place, a small "mother" hotel and houses built in varying sizes and designs within reach of it'. They had brought with them their typewriters plus paper and carbons and, according to Coward, 'bathing suits, sun-tan oil and bezique cards'. On the first morning, 3 May 1941, as Australian troops launched an ill-fated counter-attack on the Libyan port of Tobruk, the writers sat out on the beach with their backs against the sea wall. Coward described his play, coming up with names for the characters as Joyce Carey asked the occasional question. By the end of the day Coward was sure he was ready to start writing the next morning and he announced their daily schedule. Breakfast at the hotel would be followed by work from 8am till 1pm. Then there would be a break for lunch (without alcohol) followed by more writing from 2pm until 5.30 or 6pm when they would meet up and Coward would read his day's work out aloud to Joyce. 'Then bath, a drink, dinner and bed about eleven,' she recorded.

Joyce was working on a play about Keats, 'Wrestling with Fanny Brawne' as Coward dubbed it, but his work was the undoubted priority. 'In five days *Blithe Spirit* was born,' he recorded. The play opened that year and ran very successfully in London and on Broadway. A UK touring production was put together for morale-boosting purposes with Coward in the role of Charles Condomine and Joyce as his second wife Ruth.

I have been visiting Portmeirion since I was a child. In 1967 my parents took me there just after the first season of the TV series *The Prisoner* had finished filming. Also there at the time was Clough's grandson, Robin Llywelyn, only eight years old but already introduced to the writer and star of that series, Patrick McGoohan. I would have been so jealous had I known. Robin and I didn't meet then, but we have many times since. He has become a highly successful writer in the Welsh language while at the same time managing director of Portmeirion Ltd, which still runs his grandfather's village as a resort.

I've stayed in several of the cottages – my favourite is White Horses, which is directly on the sea wall and where Patrick McGoohan lived while writing, directing and starring in *The Prisoner*. But although my wife and I have walked past Anchor and Fountain, as Noël Coward's block is now known, I was unaware until recently that this was where *Blithe Spirit* was written. It's a tall building, resembling a gaunt, early nineteenth-century pub on the outside but wholly modern within. There is no plaque on the wall, just as there is no plaque to any of the other illustrious visitors who have stayed and written at Portmeirion – apart from Patrick McGoohan whose presence is recorded on the wall of White Horses. Although it attracts its fair share of celebrities, literary and otherwise, Portmeirion is still all about the village that Sir Clough created.

Since Clough Williams-Ellis' death in 1978 the world has moved a lot closer to his view of architecture, which pleases me greatly. Buildings are not just machines for living in. We need beauty. We need whimsy.

As for Noël Coward and Joyce Carey, he lived long enough to fall out of and back into fashion, while she is probably most immediately recognised today as Myrtle who runs the station café in *Brief Encounter*, Coward's bittersweet love-story so wonderfully filmed by David Lean in 1945. Joyce lived to the age of 94 and remained a close member of Coward's adopted family. Whatever happened to her play about Keats I have no idea, but Noël Coward's week at Portmeirion was highly productive. Clough's village certainly wove some magic because *Blithe Spirit* is still played all round the world today.

LONDON

GOUGH SQUARE – SAMUEL JOHNSON (1709–84)

It's surprisingly rare to sit in a room and be able to say that an author definitely paced these particular floorboards and looked through those exact windows while writing a great work of literature. So much gets replaced and refurbished and a certain amount of deduction often has to be employed if the writer hasn't kept a detailed diary. However, in the garret of 17 Gough Square, just north of London's Fleet Street, we know for certain that Dr Samuel Johnson wrote the first English dictionary over a period of eleven years with the assistance of six amanuenses who transcribed his masterly and sometimes witty definitions.

They sat at a long table (which sadly disappeared in the nineteenth century) and the great lexicographer sat at the south end of the room on his own. It's a low bare-boarded space running the width of the house that Johnson took for the specific purpose of writing the dictionary. Those floorboards we see today are original and so are the walls and window-frames. The beams supporting the roof are original too, although they are blackened now from the London Blitz. In 1940 the roof of 17 Gough Square was blown off by the Luftwaffe. Fortunately the incendiaries that followed did not destroy Dr Johnson's house – as they did the rest of the buildings nearby – because the auxiliary firemen were based downstairs.

One recent spring afternoon I sat in this lovely, sunny room at the top of many flights of wooden stairs and found it easy to imagine the doctor and his team at work here. The space has hardly changed since Johnson's time, except for the presence of a large red fire extinguisher. I couldn't begrudge the anachronism, given that the whole house once very nearly disappeared in flames.

We are fortunate that Dr Johnson's house is here at all, let alone in such good condition. Thanks must go to Cecil, First Baron Harmsworth, politician and chairman of Associated Newspapers, which had been founded by his powerful brother Lord Northcliffe. In 1911 Harmsworth and his wife bought the house in order to preserve Johnson's memory. They found No. 17 in a poor state of repair, having been a boarding house and storage facility in the nineteenth century and even taken over as annexe to the printing works next door. The Harmsworths declared that anything subsequent to Johnson must be removed and anything that was old be retained if at all possible. Fortunately a lot remained, including the painted wood panelling on the lower floors, and the front door with its mighty interior chain and iron spikes over the fanlight. The chain was to deter creditors, who often hammered on Johnson's door, and the spikes were meant to make it impossible for burglars to lower young children through the fanlight to open the door from within, apparently a common method of breaking and entering at the time.

Security might have been an issue for Dr Johnson, but his debts also kept him awake at night. He had vastly underestimated the time his dictionary would take and was running short of money. On one occasion, when he owed a small fortune for milk, he barricaded the front door with his bed so no one could carry him off to the debtors' prison in Southwark.

Photo: Adrian Mourby

Dr Johnson did not own this lovely brick house, built immediately after the Great Fire of London. He took on its lease, paying £30 a year so he would have somewhere to work on such a huge project with his team, but he also opened his house up to friends. Unfortunately they did not always get on. The blind poet Anna Williams came to live at No. 17 but took against Francis Barber, the former slave boy sent to Johnson as his valet-cum-companion soon after Johnson's wife died. Johnson refused to treat 'Frank' as a servant, and instead educated him at his own expense and effectively made him his heir. Worn down by Anna's hostility, however, the young man ran away to sea, leaving Dr Johnson to use his influence at the Admiralty to extract him.

Anna Williams probably lived on the first floor, where a remarkable pair of hinged doors allows the whole floor to be opened up into a *piano nobile* for entertainment and parties or closed to create a landing and four bedrooms. It's a brilliant piece of interior design. Johnson also gave a home here to Robert Levett, a doctor who had qualified in France but who was not allowed to practise in England. He used to minister to the poor in London's East End for free, being repaid for his services with glasses of gin. As Johnson commented on his long-term guest, 'he was the only man I know to get drunk through prudence'.

All round the house there is a feeling not only for how Johnson's household of friends and colleagues lived but also for the man himself. The tops of the balustrades have long ago lost their paint because it seems that Dr Johnson had to tap each one with his fist as he went past it, upstairs or down. Johnson was brilliant but eccentric, to put it mildly. If he missed a balustrade he had to go back to the beginning of his descent (or ascent) and start again.

My tour ended in the basement, which was where

Johnson's tea was brewed. He rarely touched alcohol but drank tea compulsively, telling a friend who reminded him he had just drunk eleven cups in a row: 'I did not count your glasses of wine, why should you number my cups of tea?' The master lexicographer feels very present in this big, baggy and ultimately very friendly house.

DOUGHTY STREET – CHARLES DICKENS (1812–70)

The Charles Dickens who moved into 48 Doughty Street was not the grizzled Victorian patriarch with that large rectangular box of a beard, but a spry Regency dandy who had just enjoyed huge success with *The Pickwick Papers* and was now working on *Oliver Twist* and *Nicholas Nickleby*.

I prefer that younger Dickens, the one whom Thomas Carlyle summed up as 'a fine little fellow' with 'clear blue intelligent eyes, eyebrows that he arches amazingly – a face of most extreme mobility ... Surmount this with a loose coil of common-coloured hair, and set it on a small compact figure'. Carlyle also commented on Dickens' extravagantly Parisian way of dressing. The young novelist, aged 25 when he moved into this terraced house in Bloomsbury, was a dandy and his house, now restored to its 1837 appearance, reflects this. The dining room (off a narrow hall) is bright blue and his drawing room on the floor above has curtains of red and gold.

Dickens and his new wife Kate lived and entertained in Doughty Street for two and a half highly productive years. They paid £80 a year in rent to the builder, who had leased the land from the Doughty family. At the time of Dickens' arrival, William IV was still on the throne. His niece, the diminutive Princess Victoria, would not become queen until the June of that year, heralding a new world where fashionable rooms became dark and cluttered with bric-a-brac (a word that entered popular English usage in the 1840s). Doughty Street therefore represents a much fresher, livelier image of Dickens than we are perhaps used to.

I walked there from Grays Inn Fields, home of the legal profession, passing through John Street and into Doughty Street past No. 58, the house occupied, after the First World War, by the writers Vera Brittain and Winifred Holtby. What Dickens called his 'town house' is at the cheaper, lower-profile end of this nineteenth-century development. It's a slim terrace with a kitchen in its basement, two main rooms on the ground floor and two above, with three bedrooms on the second floor and surmounted by an attic for servants and children.

By far the most exciting room for me was the dark red study where Dickens worked every morning. It's a large chamber with a desk, chair and bookcases that have been brought here from Gad's Hill Place in Kent, Dickens' last home. There's also a big white marble fireplace. Given that Charles Dickens was such a small man, this is a monumentally large study. Ignoring the amusement of a custodian, I paced the room, which turned out to be approximately twelve by fifteen feet with a very high ceiling.

The desk has a leather blotter raised to 45 degrees on which Dickens could write and a wastepaper basket filled with reproductions of his manuscript pages. Here was where *Oliver Twist* was written down. The window looks out on to modern housing in Brownlow Mews (Brownlow being a benevolent character in *Oliver Twist*) but I ignored the twenty-first century and imagined what it was like being Charles

Dickens, speedily writing between breakfast and lunch, and then striding off to his club or into the City of London.

The young Dickens was an energetic walker and his route to Fleet Street, home of lawyers and journalists, would have taken him through numerous courts, squares, mews and alleyways, past Dr Johnson's house in Gough Square and into Ye Olde Cheshire Cheese. I followed this route as best I could to the Cheshire Cheese, where Dickens is said to have dined on Welsh rarebit and where he set a scene from *A Tale of Two Cities*. Anthony Trollope also used this seventeenth-century pub in one of his novels, and the Rhymers' Club (a London-based group of poets that included W.B. Yeats, Ernest Dowson and Lord Alfred Douglas) often met here in the 1890s.

There is a sense of Dickens' vitality if you visit his home in Doughty Street and reconstruct his walk into Fleet Street, but there is a sad side to this house as well. In the room immediately above Dickens' study is the bedroom where Mary Hogarth, his sister-in-law, died soon after the couple moved in. The Dickens House Museum, which was established in 1925 to save the house from demolition, keeps this room as a memorial to Mary. The role of Kate's younger sister in Dickens' life was powerful, possibly too powerful. Three years younger than the new Mrs Dickens, Mary went on honeymoon with the couple and also moved with them to Doughty Street in 1837, dying the same year.

It was an event from which the writer never recovered, and his sentimental depiction of innocent, pre-sexual women (Rose Maylie, Kate Nickleby, Agnes Wickfield and Little Nell) is one of the weaknesses in Dickens' output. How poor Kate Dickens felt about her beatified younger sister as she herself grew older, fatter, neglected, and depressed has been much written about.

Photo: Spudgun67

At 48 Doughty Street the visitor not only sees where Charles Dickens lived and wrote, but also where he became the Dickens phenomenon, a supremely successful, busy, charismatic London novelist whose work is shot through with sentimentality, and the love of young women too good for this world.

THE SAVOY HOTEL – OSCAR WILDE (1854–1900)

There can be few matches of personality and surroundings as perfect as that of Oscar Wilde and London's Savoy Hotel. Both represented conspicuous levels of luxury allied with modern innovation and taste. In 1889 the Savoy was London's first hotel to provide electric lights in every bedroom and baths in the majority. It also boasted an electric lift. At the same time, the Irish dramatist Oscar Wilde was critiquing the wealthy English in a series of modern West End comedies that hid their sting in the laughter. After the success of *Lady Windermere's Fan* in 1892 Wilde was commissioned to write a new play, which he called *A Woman of No Importance*, for the Haymarket Theatre. He completed it in Norfolk while staying with his young lover, Lord Alfred Douglas. On 2 March 1893 Wilde moved into the Savoy so he could be nearby for rehearsals.

The Savoy had been built in 1889 by the theatrical impresario Richard D'Oyly Carte, using profits from his productions of Gilbert and Sullivan operettas. Both composer and librettist had shares in the hotel, which was adjacent to the theatre in which their Savoyard operas were premiered. Carte hired César Ritz as manager and Auguste Escoffier as chef de cuisine.

Richard D'Oyly Carte already knew his famous guest well. In 1882 he had cannily paid for Wilde to give a lecture tour across the United States to prepare Americans for the Gilbert and Sullivan operetta *Patience*, which parodied Wilde's Aesthetic Movement.

We know from some bills that came to light in the 1980s that Wilde's first suite comprised rooms 361 and 362 (modern room numbers 302/304), for which he seems to have paid a guinea a night. His sitting rooms and bedroom at the north-west corner of the hotel overlooked Carting Lane, which is where the main entrance to the Savoy Theatre was situated at that time. On 8 March, however, Oscar moved down the corridor into rooms 343/346 (modern Suite 314) at the south-west corner of the hotel. Here he had a wide balcony overlooking the Thames – the very view of Waterloo Bridge that Monet would paint over and over again ten years later when he stayed at the Savoy.

This suite had a private bathroom and cost him two guineas a night. My guess is that the move was occasioned by the arrival of Lord Alfred. At his trial two years later, Wilde told Sir Edward Carson that he had lived at the Savoy with Lord Alfred for a month. After adding in their meals and champagne, Wilde was soon complaining that he had run up a bill of £49 in just one week.

During this time Wilde was attending rehearsals of *A Woman of No Importance* and rewriting where necessary. Although he cultivated an image of effortless wit, Oscar Wilde was a highly conscientious craftsman, applying himself to his art and to crafting his public persona. In both, he endeavoured to shroud his seriousness of purpose in humour. Like the Savoy itself, Wilde was glamour on the surface but a lot of hard work behind the scenes.

I've only stayed once at the Savoy, but I've visited its

Courtesy of The Savoy

American Bar frequently. This, one of the first cocktail bars in London, was given an Art Deco makeover in the late 1920s and retains a brittle glamour. You half expect to see Cole Porter at the piano. Among the American literary greats who have eased themselves onto barstools and into armchairs here are Ernest Hemingway (of course), Edgar Wallace, H.L. Mencken and Sinclair Lewis, whom Hemingway detested and who married the journalist Dorothy Thompson while staying at the Savoy. The British contingent are represented by George Bernard Shaw, the Sitwells and Arnold Bennett – who loved the place so much he based two of his novels, *Grand Hotel Babylon* (1902) and *Imperial Palace* (1930), on the Savoy. More recently the hotel – and by extension its bar – has even had its own writers-in-residence: lucky Fay Weldon, Kathy Lette, Frank McCourt and Michael Morpurgo.

After sitting on my barstool for half an hour – I get a disproportionate amount of pleasure from watching bartenders at work – I was collected by the duty manager and shown upstairs. We used the red lift which – though modern – occupies the shaft of the first lift D'Oyly Carte installed. It was built big enough to accommodate a chaise for the comfort of guests – and has a small sofa in it today.

The third floor, like so much of the hotel, has been refurbished in a twenty-first-century Art Deco style with relatively low ceilings and bright lights. Oscar's second set of rooms were occupied but his first rooms, opposite the old theatre entrance, were free. Room 302 is tucked into a discreet corner. We peeped in. It had an attractive bay window but was inoffensively decorated with original but unremarkable art on the wall. Only a photo of Oscar on the chest of drawers gave any hint of his occupancy.

I stood there thinking about the difficult time poor Wilde had with the volatile Lord Alfred while at the Savoy. At the end of his month's residence, he wrote: 'I fear I must leave; no money, no credit, and a heart of lead.' Three years later at the time of his bankruptcy in 1895, Wilde still owed the Savoy £86.

Obviously the size of this bill preoccupied him. In *The Importance of Being Earnest*, which Wilde wrote the same year as his trial, there is a scene (often cut) where a solicitor turns up to serve a writ on Mr Ernest Worthing 'for debts owed to The Savoy Hotel Co. Limited, being a sum in excess of £700'.

Oscar Wilde is sometimes seen as a gay martyr these days. While he was vindictively judged as the result of his association with Lord Alfred Douglas, I'd prefer to remember him not as a victim, but as a man who enjoyed the very best in life while he could, and I'm sure Wilde would want this too. A five-minute walk down the Strand from the Savoy Hotel there is a memorial to him in Adelaide Street. The old fellow is looking a bit raddled as he reclines on his plinth, but the inscription says it all: 'We are all in the gutter, but some of us are looking at the stars.'

BROWN'S HOTEL, ALBEMARLE STREET – RUDYARD KIPLING (1865–1936)

Brown's in Albemarle Street is one of London's gracious hotel dames. It's been open since 1837, when over the period of a year Lord Byron's former butler, James Brown, bought up four London townhouses in Dover Street to create a gentleman's hotel. A later owner of Brown's then knocked through to St George's Hotel on Albemarle Street to create Brown's and St George's Hotel, which eventually spread over eleven houses. Today the hotel is a rich warren of history with its corridors sloping to accommodate the shift between floor levels of all the different buildings.

Many writers have stayed here in this discreet, friendly hotel, including Oscar Wilde, Arthur Conan Doyle, Robert Louis Stevenson, J.M. Barrie, Bram Stoker and Agatha Christie. Winston Churchill, no mean writer himself, once opined: 'When in London I do not stay at a hotel, I stay at Brown's.'

The writer most celebrated by the hotel, however, is Rudyard Kipling, who spent the first night of his honeymoon here in 1892. Henry James gave away the bride, Carrie Balestier, at All Souls church, Langham Place, half a mile north of the hotel. Kipling recorded that they were married in the 'thick of an influenza epidemic, when the undertakers had run out of black horses and the dead had to be content with brown ones'.

Rudyard Kipling often returned to Brown's. He completed the last of the stories for his *Jungle Book* here in 1894. At the time he was living with his wife and children in the United States, having built a house in Vermont, but Mr Kipling needed to be in London to oversee the publication by Macmillan of his Indian stories for children. Although Kipling is now best known for this book – thanks in part to the Disney cartoon and a number of other film adaptations – his writing for adults was much more highly regarded in his lifetime. It's often forgotten these days that in 1907 Rudyard Kipling was the first English-language recipient of the Nobel Prize for Literature. Meanwhile Brown's, with its central location off Piccadilly and easy-going comforts, developed a good reputation among authors. It was near the best shops and the best clubs and not far from offices of the major publishing houses. When Mark Twain stayed here he scandalised a reporter from *The Times* by appearing in the lobby in his blue bathrobe to answer journalists' questions.

Brown's was so much Kipling's residence in town that he even answered his correspondence from here. A typed letter now on display in the hotel shows him dealing with a land issue in East Sussex, where he lived from 1902 until his death. Having typed Brown's address at the top of the page on 5 March 1919, Mr Kipling explains to a Mr Shepherd that he is reluctant to rent out the land in Rottingdean as an allotment because the Kipling family hope soon to sell it. The letter has nothing to do with the world of literature, but it's proof the author was here and conducted his daily business from Brown's.

On the night of 12 January 1936 Kipling was working on his memoir, *Something of Myself (for my Friends Known and Unknown)*, when he was found slumped over the desk in his room at Brown's with a perforated duodenal ulcer. He underwent surgery, but died less than a week later on 18 January at the age of 70. The pallbearers at his funeral included Prime Minister Stanley Baldwin, Kipling's cousin.

I stayed at Brown's recently, as the designer Olga Polizzi had just refurbished its Kipling Suite in his honour, and I was invited to see it. As no hotel guestbooks have survived from the period before the Second World War, it isn't known in which rooms he actually stayed and wrote his memoirs, *The Jungle Book*, or indeed his letters to Mr Shepherd of Rottingdean. Instead, the hotel has put together a suite of rooms overlooking Albemarle Street in memory of him. There are photos of Kipling and lots of his books on display. A plaster monkey hangs, almost unobserved, by the main door into the suite as a deft reference to *The Jungle Book*. There is also a bust of Lord Byron in the drawing room. Byron, who died long before Brown's even opened, appears in various places around the hotel, rather like its patron saint.

Photo: © Kate Tadman-Mourby

The actual desk at which Kipling collapsed in 1936 is not in this suite but on the other side of the hotel, in the Dover Suite, which overlooks Dover Street within the original part of the hotel. Maybe Ms Polizzi thought it ghoulish to have the desk at which Kipling's duodenal ulcer perforated on display in a suite bearing his name. (It's certainly far less useful than the spacious modern table she has provided instead.) The original is a low, kidney-shaped desk in dark polished wood with hardly room to fit a modern pair of legs under it. I sat there nevertheless and imagined him typing away here. No space for the stacks of reference books and coffee cups that many of us pile up when working. Mr Kipling must have been a very orderly, very focused writer. But then his prolific output rather suggests that.

OXFORD

CHRIST CHURCH – LEWIS CARROLL (1832–98)

Oxford, a very real city, one hour up the M40 from London, has inspired an extraordinary number of fantasy writers. Charles Lutwidge Dodgson (aka Lewis Carroll) wrote about Alice Liddell's adventures down a rabbit hole and through a looking glass in Oxford. Clive Staples Lewis (aka C.S. Lewis) invented Narnia here, and John (J.R.R.) Tolkien created Middle Earth. More recently Philip Pullman found a parallel universe between the hornbeams on Oxford's Sunderland Avenue in his *Dark Materials* trilogy. Only Colin Dexter with his Inspector Morse crime novels has reflected the everyday reality of Oxford, a city of sexual intrigue, gluttony and murder.

Being based in Oxford for the last fifteen years, I'm aware of the paradox that most of the authors who live here could write about this fascinating city but instead prefer to disappear down their own rabbit holes. It seems to be the mathematician Charles Lutwidge Dodgson who started this trend with *Alice's Adventures Underground*, which he changed to *Alice in Wonderland* when the story was published in 1865 under his pen name, Lewis Carroll.

Carroll lived and worked at Christ Church, one of the largest of Oxford's colleges. It sits on St Aldate's, a street that runs down towards the Thames. The college was built by Cardinal Wolsey, Henry VIII's chief minister at the time

Photo: © Kate Tadman-Mourby

when he was trying to arrange the king's divorce from his first queen, Catherine. Initially known as Cardinal College, it was renamed King Henry VIII's College after 1529 when Wolsey fell disastrously from favour. Finally in 1546 it was refounded by Henry as Christ Church.

When I was a student, Christ Church was renowned, even among those of us not studying at Oxford, as the 'heartiest' of English colleges. Allegedly, while most Oxford colleges raided a rival, throwing their beds out of windows as a prank, the wealthy students of Christ Church were so thick that they simply threw their own beds out of the windows. Perhaps in Dodgson's day undergraduates were not quite so silly – after all, Christ Church has produced more British prime ministers than any other college in Oxford or Cambridge.

It was a bright May morning when I paid my entrance fee. All Oxford colleges admit visitors on selected days but after the success of the first Harry Potter films – in which Christ Church's Great Hall doubled as Hogwarts – this was one of the first to charge admission.

The bowler-hatted 'bulldog' (custodian) who showed me round was tired of people hoping to find Snape and Dumbledore at Christ Church and was positively happy (bulldogs rarely smile) that I'd come here in search of Carroll. He pointed up to one of the windows of the Great Hall that is dedicated to the author and which contains a portrait of Alice Liddell.

Alice was one of the daughters of Henry Liddell, Dean of Christ Church, and at the age of four she captured the attention of the middle-aged don Carroll, who was a keen photographer. A picture of her at the age of seven by Carroll shows a child with an unusual amount going on behind her eyes. A later portrait by Julia Margaret Cameron of Alice as a young woman suggests restless discontent.

Also in the Great Hall I was shown the fire grate supported by two human figures with elongated necks. They are said to be the inspiration for Alice's potion-induced long neck in Wonderland. Behind High Table I saw a panelled door concealing a narrow spiral staircase by which academics could suddenly disappear, like rabbits, downstairs.

When I asked if it were possible to see Lewis Carroll's actual rooms, the bulldog shook his head and just nodded towards the north-west corner of Tom Quad. This is a working college still and those rooms, overlooking St Aldate's, are always occupied by an academic, who probably does not see their role as part of the tourist trail. Instead, I was shown Dean Liddell's gardens where there is a voluminous chestnut tree. Evidently Alice's real cat Dinah used to seat herself in it in a most Cheshire Cat-like way. From here there is a door into the beautiful Cathedral Garden, which was always kept locked because little girls were not allowed to play in there. Alice however could see into it from the nursery, something else that might have inspired Lewis Carroll's inaccessible garden in Wonderland.

On my way out I called into the small shop at No. 83 St Aldate's, which is now known as Alice's Shop. This name is not only derived from its shelves of Wonderland merchandise. Here behind a red wooden door was the sweet shop where Alice Liddell would buy her barley sugars. The shopkeeper at the time, an old lady wrapped in a shawl, apparently reminded Alice of a sheep and she confided this, like so much else, to Carroll. The sheep-shopkeeper crops up in one of the more surreal sections of *Through the Looking Glass*.

The more you know about Lewis Carroll's Oxford the more you realise his Alice stories are an eccentric tapestry woven out of the threads of her life – and his own. Carroll put himself and his friend Duckworth into Wonderland as the Duck and the Dodo (a pun on the stuttering Do-Do-Dodgson's name). At the Museum of Natural History on Parks Road you can even see one of the few stuffed dodos in Europe, a bird that Alice and Carroll would have visited.

Ultimately, however, these sources of inspiration fail to decode Alice's adventures. The books themselves defy explanation, but it can be great fun spotting the raw material that was reworked in Lewis Carroll's remarkable imagination for his favourite audience. I didn't see his college rooms but I definitely saw the city that inspired him.

THE EAGLE AND CHILD – J.R.R. TOLKIEN (1892–1973)

Many years ago I took my friend Jeremy for a drink in Oxford on the eve of his wedding. I was to be his best man the next day and felt I should offer some kind of stag night. We met up at the Eagle and Child, a narrow inn on St Giles dating back to at least the English Civil War, and I bought us both pints. We sat in one of the tiny front parlours where on a busy day you rub knees with the other drinkers, so close are the tables. After we had finished our beers my old school friend announced that he had to leave for dinner with his parents. That was the end of what became known thereafter as Jeremy's Stag Half-Hour.

Coming back to the Eagle and Child many years later on J.R.R. Tolkien's birthday, I noticed few changes. It's one of those English pubs where alteration, let alone refurbishment, is anathema. The most obvious innovation was a large painted portrait of the *Lord of the Rings* author over the small Victorian fireplace in the parlour where we'd sat in the early 1990s. There was a matching portrait of C.S. Lewis in the equally small parlour on the other side of the pub's narrow vestibule. Tolkien and 'Jack' Lewis, good friends and colleagues in real life, fellow creators of fantasy worlds, are a partnership in Oxford tourism today. At Magdalen College you can stroll along Addison's Walk, a triangular route named after an eighteenth-century college Fellow, which they took together when Lewis was grappling with converting back from atheism to Christianity.

The Eastgate Hotel, lying between Lewis at Magdalen and Tolkien at Merton College, is one of many drinking places that hosted the writers, usually for a Monday morning pint.

But the Eagle and Child (also known locally as the 'Bird and Baby'), was where Tolkien and Lewis would meet their fellow 'Inklings' on Tuesdays in a back room behind the bar. They met in the Rabbit Room where they would read and discuss each other's work. Tolkien, a purist whose Middle Earth was essentially Anglo-Saxon, would despair of Lewis' habit of yoking in characters from every era and world culture for his Narnia novels.

So recently on a wet Tuesday in January at noon I made my way to the Rabbit Room of the Bird and Baby, and ordered a half-pint of real ale in memory of my own Oxford friend. A new sign by the bar quoted from Pippin and Merry in the first film in Peter Jackson's *Lord of the Rings* trilogy:

What's that?
This, my friend, is a pint.
It comes in pints? I'm getting one.

I, however, was here only to catch some hint of Tolkien, not to get as drunk as a hobbit. While waiting for my half to pour, I occupied myself looking round the Rabbit

Photo: Ozeye

Room. The partitioning has been removed since the 1940s, making it more of a corner of the bar now. Black and white photos of Tolkien and Lewis are framed on the walls, along with images of Oxford in their time. There are two long tables, a fireplace, a commemorative plaque and a few books. On a wet day like today it was easy to imagine a group of middle-aged Oxford dons squeezing in together, their tweed jackets steaming slightly as they dried off in front of the coal fire.

It's less easy to imagine Tolkien finding anything of the grandeur of Middle Earth in the Eagle and Child, although he did write scenes in the Prancing Pony, the Green Dragon and the Golden Perch, which definitely have something of the dark, clutter and noise of these small wood-panelled rooms.

A half of warm British beer lasts no time at all, so in a break between downpours I got back on my bike and wondered where to head next in pursuit of J.R.R. The Inklings also met across the road at the Lamb and Flag. Lewis and Tolkien seemed to convene anywhere a pint could be poured but instead I headed into the centre of Oxford and its medieval colleges.

I could have visited Merton, where Tolkien was Professor of English Language and Literature for twelve years until his retirement and move to genteel Bournemouth, but Magdalen College lets you in for free if you're a local. It also has a medieval tower overlooking the River Cherwell and a gift shop selling C.S. Lewis memorabilia which I enjoyed browsing.

This was the home of Tolkien's literary comrade – even though the relationship cooled in the 1950s after Lewis married without telling any of his friends. The college grounds are extensive, like those of a British stately home, and extend to an island in the River Cherwell on which runs

Addison's Walk. It's lined with so many trees that in summer it can resemble a dark tunnel. The Tolkien Society claims that Addison's Walk may have inspired his depiction of Mirkwood. Certainly the stumps of dead trees that have been carved into chairs have a Middle Earth quality about them.

I completed a circuit – if indeed triangles have circuits – and then the rains blew back in again. I stood under a leafless tree and wondered like Bilbo, sheltering in the goblin cave, why I had ever left my warm hobbit-home. I could cycle to 20 Northmoor Road now, Tolkien's house where, while marking examination papers, he wrote down the words: 'In a hole in the ground there lived a hobbit.' Or I could cycle as far as the Wolvercote Cemetery and Tolkien's grave. Both were suitable acts of pilgrimage, but the house is in private hands and the grave was over three miles of rain away. So in the end I went back to the Bird and Baby and ordered a pint this time and drank another toast to Tolkien and his friend C.S. Lewis, and to my friend Jeremy who had died – ridiculously young – the previous autumn.

KELMSCOTT MANOR, OXFORDSHIRE – WILLIAM MORRIS (1834–96)

There can be few writer residences as satisfying as Kelmscott Manor in Oxfordshire, where William Morris lived from 1871 until his death. Yet it is one almost wholly without revelations. We want a bit of a surprise when we visit a writer's room, I think. We want to learn something unexpected.

Morris, a man of remarkable energies, threw himself into his life, working as an artist, designer, poet, novelist,

Photo: Daderot

110

translator and printer. While Thomas Hardy and Gerard Manley Hopkins – his almost exact contemporaries – took the novel and poetry towards Modernism, Morris took Britain back to the misty Middle Ages.

Kelmscott Manor, built in 1570, looks like a setting for one of Morris' books. The polymath did most of his writing here, having given up painting by 1862. Among books written at Kelmscott were *The Story of Sigurd the Volsung* (1877), *Hopes and Fears for Art* (1882), *A Tale of the House of the Wolfings* (1889), *Poems by the Way* (1891), *News from Nowhere* (1890) and *The Wood Beyond the World* (1894). He also wrote a number of translations – *The Odyssey, The Aeneid, Beowulf* and *Old French Romances*. His work was widely read. These days, when the words 'William Morris' are almost always followed by 'design', 'style' or 'wallpaper', it is salutary to realise that in his lifetime Morris was better known as a writer.

William Morris' pursuit of a purer world that looked medieval but practised socialism was helped by his being born into a wealthy family. He could afford to follow his dreams and live where he wanted. Morris was accompanied on these adventures by his wife Jane, whose beauty he fell for while a student at Oxford, and by the poet and painter Dante Gabriel Rossetti, who spent most of his adult life in love with Jane and was incapable of painting any subject well apart from her. Jane Morris became the face of Pre-Raphaelite beauty. Her large dark eyes, long nose, full lips and resolute chin can be seen everywhere in Victorian art, in book illustrations, in paintings, even in stained glass. The ideal – for both men and women – was to look like Jane Morris. Thanks to the adoration she inspired in the Pre-Raphaelite movement, there are even graphics accompanying newspaper reports of the Boer War in South Africa in which the heroic young subalterns all look like Jane.

Theirs was a strange ménage. By the time the three of them arrived at Kelmscott Manor, Morris had already built the innovatory neo-Gothic Red House in Kent and moved from there to Queen Square in Bloomsbury, where his design business, Morris & Co., prospered. He then decided he wanted to bring his children up in the country. Kelmscott, a limestone Elizabethan manor house, was perfect and he took a joint tenancy with Rossetti.

Arriving at Kelmscott the day the RAF were doing a series of public displays at nearby Brize Norton, I couldn't miss the dramatic contrast between the Red Arrows overhead and the pink roses over William Morris' door, disturbing his medieval idyll. The house is owned by the Society of Antiquaries and it's opened only on Wednesdays and Saturdays. After Morris' death Jane Morris bought Kelmscott and offered to leave it to Oxford University if they would preserve it as a museum. The university declined so it went to the Antiquaries.

Inside the manor house were pictures and decorative works by Morris, Burne-Jones and Rossetti as well as Philip Webb (architect of the Red House). The whole building looked like a showcase for William Morris design in its furniture, textiles, paintings, carpets and ceramics. The walls were covered with Morris' take on medieval tapestries, and the four-poster beds were draped with them too. His trellis wallpaper and oakleaf motif fabrics were everywhere. Looking at the fireplaces and casements that had not been modified by Morris, I got the feeling that when he moved in, the house might have resembled a nineteenth-century vicarage out of George Eliot but the Morrises took it back to Chaucer's time.

It was all very pretty and full of people recognising the originals of their cushion covers or curtains, but it was just what I expected. The only surprising element was in the outhouses where my wife and I found a converted farm building containing a triple lavatory where three people could sit simultaneously. With or without plumbing (I did not check).

Of all of Morris' design innovations this was the most unlikely. It was difficult to imagine it being used by this middle-class Victorian household so I found it particularly delightful to come across a caricature that Osbert Lancaster had penned of Rossetti, Jane and Morris sitting on the lavatories, the men with their trousers round their ankles and Morris furrowing his brow as he tries to read *La Roumant de la Rose* in the original French.

William Morris has become one of those great unread writers now, like Charles Kingsley and Vita Sackville-West. He achieved a remarkable amount in his 62 years. In addition to his writings and design business, he founded the Society for the Protection of Ancient Buildings to guard against the philistinism that accompanied Victorian notions of progress. He founded the Socialist League to work for greater social justice, and the Kelmscott Press to publish beautifully-illustrated limited-edition books. And of course he gave us the 'William Morris' look, which still sells around the world.

Before we left I bought a William Morris mug lettered with one of his best known declarations. 'Have nothing in your houses that you do not know to be useful, or believe to be beautiful.' Prescient words at a time of Victorian clutter and worth remembering today. But tellingly I did not buy a copy of *Hopes and Fears for Art* in which Morris made that statement.

I hoped he'd forgive me.

EDINBURGH

HERIOT ROW – ROBERT LOUIS STEVENSON (1850–94)

There's no mistaking the house where the author of *Treasure Island* grew up in Edinburgh's neoclassical New Town. Chiselled into the sandstone are the words 'The home of Robert Louis Stevenson 1857–1880' and next to the large red door an old brass plate reminds you that this is a private house, 'Not A Museum'.

Fortunately 17 Heriot Row is also a B&B run by a bearded gentleman and his wife who glory – can there be any other verb for it? – in the names of John and Felicitas Macfie. Mr Macfie is the eleventh owner of this triple-bayed, terraced house built in 1808. The sixth owner was Thomas Stevenson, father of Robert Louis. The Stevenson family arrived here in 1857 when their only child Robert was six years old. It was hoped that this south-facing house on higher ground would be better for Stevenson's young wife and son, both of whom were prone to chest infections.

A devoted father, Mr Stevenson had the roof level of the house raised so that his only child would have two spacious, sunny rooms on the second floor, one as the day nursery and the other as the night nursery. There would also be a comfortable room for Robert's nanny at the rear of the house. This is now one of the rooms that Mr Macfie lets out to paying guests with two single beds and an en-suite shower.

Down below, the room where Robert's parents slept is also available to guests. It has an en-suite bath that was installed after young Robert married in 1880 because his American wife thought it antiquated to carry pails of hot water through the house. According to Mr Macfie, the redoubtable Fanny Matilda Van de Grift Osbourne Stevenson teased her father-in-law about his parsimony for not installing a modern bathroom – and the tactic worked. Thomas Stevenson, a successful designer of lighthouses, not only installed a panelled-in bath that guests use to this day but a cold water shower over it (also still working).

Mr Macfie told me all this as we sat drinking tea in the massive red dining room at the front of Stevenson House. When he and his wife redecorated No. 17, they stripped off ten layers of paint and discovered that the wood panelling of the house would have been brightly coloured in the mid-nineteenth century. Some walls were even painted a dazzling yellow. Sepia photography does not do justice to how garishly the Victorians decorated. They had access to aniline dyes – fuchsia, Magdala red, Tyrian purple, Martius yellow, bleu de Paris and aldehyde green – that simply could not be mixed in Jane Austen's pastel time.

After drinking our tea we went upstairs to see Mrs Stevenson's drawing room overlooking Heriot Row. The hall and stairs are lit from an oval skylight in the roof and are wonderfully spacious, but then they were public areas for visitors to traverse, far more so than today when we invariably receive visitors on the ground floor.

At the top of a flight of stairs lined with swords, a large wooden door opens into the drawing room which runs the width of the house. Here the sixteen-year-old Robert, listening to his mother and her friends decry the behaviour of young people today, interjected from the shadows, 'I'm not as black as I'm painted'. One of them returned home to declare she had just met a young poet, a Heinrich Heine with a Scottish accent who 'talked as Charles Lamb wrote'.

We then went to the topmost floor to see the bedroom of Alison Cunningham (known as Cummy), the nanny to whom Robert dictated his childhood stories. Up here was Stevenson's own bedroom and the day nursery where as a teenager he wrote some of his earliest works, including *The Pentland Rising*, which was privately published by his father when he was sixteen.

Later, after Robert Louis Stevenson had fallen out with his parents and married Fanny, a divorcée, against their will, he returned to this house with his new wife and she helped effect a reconciliation between parents and beloved son. The newly-married Mr and Mrs Robert L. Stevenson would have stayed in his old rooms at the front of the house and Mr Macfie is sure that parts of *Treasure Island* were written in the old day nursery. So I was excited to see where one of the most gripping books of my childhood had been created.

However, when the door swung open what I saw was the bedroom of Mr Macfie's twin daughters, looking as such rooms often do. My host tried to explain where the book shelves would have been and how Robert Louis Stevenson had trunks full of more books stacked against the windows, but I just couldn't see past the clutter of contemporary childhood.

Later in Edinburgh's Writers' Museum I saw Stevenson's riding boots, the shell and silver ring given to him by a grateful Samoan chief at the end of Stevenson's travelling life, and a wardrobe made by Deacon Brodie (the inspiration for *Dr Jekyll and Mr Hyde*) that used to stand in the nursery and which may have inspired the young writer. But I couldn't help thinking of that room full of mattresses, Playmobil and cuddly toys.

THE ELEPHANT HOUSE – J.K. ROWLING (B. 1965)

Tables in Edinburgh where J.K. Rowling sat and wrote *Harry Potter* are becoming as ubiquitous as beds in which Queen Elizabeth I slept and bars in which Hemingway drank. The author has gone on the record about two Edinburgh locations, however. One of the best-selling novelists of her generation began the Harry Potter series in The Elephant House café on George IV Bridge and ended it at the Balmoral Hotel.

The Elephant House is in one of those big, dark Edinburgh buildings that seem to extend over an infinite number of floors above and below street level. A large faded sign on its exterior wall reads Harvey's Furniture Show Rooms. In 1995 a café opened here with a large carved elephant chair, a cabinet of miniature elephants and elephants stencilled round the mirrors. It was inside this that the newly divorced, unpublished author would bring her daughter in a pram. The myth that J.K. Rowling wrote in cafés to avoid heating her flat has been quashed by the author. She used the pram ride to lull her child to sleep. Then she could park the two of them at the back of this bright bohemian café and write overlooking Greyfriars churchyard.

Visiting The Elephant House today it's clear that the café is proud of its unique identity, with Elephant T-shirts for sale at the end of the long counter, but a few cuttings on the notice boards reinforce the Rowling connection, and there is a sign in the window that reads 'The Elephant House, "Birthplace" of Harry Potter'. The same claim is made in Mandarin underneath. Chinese tourists love to stand outside and block up the wide pavement as they take selfies and groupies.

The café is rarely quiet. The noise of the coffee grinder, the hubbub of voices and the sound of traffic every time the door swings open blend into a wall of noise within which it is surprisingly easy to concentrate. I write in cafés myself. In this one you get your coffee and pastries at a counter and are then supposed to wait to be seated, but every time I've visited, the staff have been too busy behind the counter. So it's easy enough to walk through to the back room and aim for the table with the metal 'reserved' sign which is where, as she recorded in a TV programme, J.K. sat whenever she could. There's no plaque on the wall, however, nor anything as obvious as the large arrow hanging from the ceiling in Katz's Deli in New York pointing to where Harry and Sally discussed female orgasms. The only permanent form of commemoration for one of the most successful book series of the late twentieth century is in the small lavatories nearby. They are covered in graffiti: 'Harry, yer a wizard', 'Dobby is a Free Elf' and '"Let me Slytherin," said Draco Malfoy to Hermione'. The owners have long ago given up painting over the scrawls that cover the walls, mirrors and windows.

On my way out I noticed a signed first edition of the first Harry Potter novel inside the glass case containing elephants. But on the whole, the Rowling connection is low-key. Who knows what other novels are being written there now?

On the other side of the massive North Bridge, opened in 1897 to link Edinburgh's Old and New Towns, stands the Balmoral Hotel, originally the North British Station Hotel, a massive fortress of a Victorian hotel built to service the Waverley Station below. Here in Room 552, now the J.K. Rowling Suite, is where the last of those Harry Potter novels was completed, behind a door which in her honour now has an owl door knocker – unlike the other 187 hotel rooms.

Photo: Adrian Mourby

Inside is a living room and bedroom in light blue with views up to Calton Hill and a Jack Vettriano print over the bed. There's also a marble bust of Hermes on which the author recorded, 'Finished writing *Harry Potter and the Deathly Hallows* in this room (552) on 11 January 2007'. I doubt that most guests have their graffiti preserved in this way. The desk at which the author sat has been preserved in situ, but there's not much else of Potter or Rowling apart from the complete novels with their multi-coloured spines on a small shelf below some baronial-looking antlers. The room is fully booked for the foreseeable future. I was only able to see it in the brief window after housekeeping had been in and just before the next literary pilgrims arrived.

On my way out of the Balmoral I called in at the lovely Palm Court lounge where afternoon tea is taken these days as a harpist plays amid the tall white Corinthian columns. 'J.K. Rowling used to write here,' said the woman who showed me to my table, 'usually at that table facing the mirrors. She liked how old they were' (they are indeed) 'and she preferred to face them because it was less distracting than facing into the room.'

Truly J.K. Rowling did write everywhere.

THE CHANNEL ISLANDS

HAUTEVILLE HOUSE, ST PETER PORT, GUERNSEY – VICTOR HUGO (1802–85)

You never know quite what to expect when tracking a writer down to their lair. Some authors like to surround themselves with luxury, while some border on the ascetic, expunging all distractions from their surroundings, but nowhere surprised me quite like the home that Victor Hugo constructed for himself on the island of Guernsey. Externally it is an ordinary-looking, tall, double-fronted early nineteenth-century family house in the respectable neighbourhood of Hauteville Street. Inside, however, it's a work of art, dramatic and highly eclectic in its style, by turns neo-Gothic, Louis XV and Chinese.

After labouring up the hill I was shown around by a young French curator – the house was donated to the city of Paris by Hugo's descendants – who went to great lengths to interpret every room for me, seeing symbolism in the smallest detail. I was told that the fact that the ground floor was dark but the top floor where Hugo wrote was very light reflected the progress of humanity from ignorance and shadows, up to illumination and clarity. It might also have had something to do with the fact that each ground-floor room was lit by a relatively small window, while on the roofline Hugo was able to build a steel and glass conservatory, but I said nothing.

The author came to Guernsey in 1855. He had been living

in exile on Jersey but had just been expelled, along with a number of others, for a letter that was critical of Queen Victoria. Victor Hugo was 53 and already the successful author of four novels including *Notre-Dame de Paris*, ten plays – two of which had been turned into operas by Verdi – and various volumes of poetry. But it was the runaway success of his volume of new autobiographical verse *Les Contemplations* in 1856 that made him a wealthy man and allowed him to buy 38 Hauteville Street. It also gave Hugo the income to decorate it as he wished. '*Contemplations* will pay for everything!' he announced.

Guided tours around the house start on the ground floor in the Billiard Room, which is darkly panelled and decorated with formal paintings of the Hugo family. It's only when you pass into the Tapestry Room that the audacity of Hugo's ambition is revealed. He scoured Guernsey for antiques, including over 60 carved wooden chests that he cannibalised to panel the interior of the house. In this gloomy room there is not a piece of wall or ceiling that isn't covered with either tapestry or carved wood. It is like the setting for some Gothic novel but full of didactic Hugo statements. On either side of the fireplace are carved the names of those Hugo considered the 'geniuses of society', including Moses, Socrates, Columbus, Shakespeare and George Washington. Behind a panel is revealed Hugo's darkroom where he and others developed daguerreotypes (Victor Hugo really liked being photographed).

Across a corridor whose walls and ceiling are covered with dinner plates stands Hugo's dining room, which is decorated with hundreds of Chinese tiles. The fireplace itself is in the shape of a huge 'H' which my curator friend insisted was not vanity and might have stood for Hauteville or even Humanity. I wasn't convinced. A throne that Hugo called the Ancestor Chair dominates the dining table. It has the names of Hugo's father on one arm and that of his earliest ancestor, 'Georges 1534' on the other. I was told that a chain across the chair indicated that it was only to be sat on by ancestors. Hugo was aware that sixteenth-century Georges was fictional but throughout the house he never let the truth get in the way of a good story. At the top of the chair the motto is spelled out: EGO HUGO. The house seemed to have the word 'MOI!' stamped on just about every surface.

Ascending the stairs, dramatically lit from a skylight, one comes to the Red Drawing Room and the Blue Drawing Room. The Red is very red indeed and its north-eastern wall is decorated with four life-sized gold-painted Chinese figures that were said to have come from the *Bucentaur*, the state barge of the doges of Venice. They didn't, but again Hugo encouraged the story. The adjoining Blue Drawing Room is similarly oriental in style and as blue as the Red Room is red. The bedrooms of Hugo's wife and daughter are also on this floor but because they preferred to sleep in rooms of a less idiosyncratic – and perhaps actually more restful – style, the city of Paris has not preserved their decor and now uses them as offices.

Up on the second floor is the Oak Gallery, which is full of even more recycled panelling and is dominated by a great wooden candelabra that Hugo designed using old bobbins as candleholders. 'It's a pity I'm a poet,' he wrote. 'What an architect I would have made!' A table at its west end is presided over by three chairs. The word PATER is spelled out in brass studs on the middle one. These chairs face the red so-called Garibaldi Bed, which is housed in an absolutely enormous four poster frame. But Hugo's Italian hero did not sleep here. The author invited him several times to Guernsey but the revolutionary never arrived. That didn't have to get in the way of naming the bed, however.

Across the corridor lie the bedrooms of Hugo's sons, which are too dull to be open to the public, but the corridor itself is interesting because it is completely lined with books. Victor Hugo said he liked books but disliked any kind of reading room or library and so the idea was that you took a book from shelves in the corridor and took it off to read wherever you wished.

The topmost floor is the most interesting but the least pyrotechnic of all. In 1856 Hugo moved the housemaids out into the basement and turned this garret into his own modest Chinese-style bedroom and his first writing room, which he called the Antechamber. Here in the middle of this low corridor between the bedrooms Hugo wrote *Les Misérables*, standing at a desk that faced out of the attic window. In 1862, with his masterpiece finally completed, he extended a conservatory-style room out across the roof to create what he dubbed 'The Look Out'. It still has great views across the sea to France and in the corner a hinged flap on the wall can be raised to create a writing table.

This was where Hugo wrote his Guernsey novel, *Les Travailleurs de la mer* (Toilers of the Sea). It's an odd book full of stormy weather and betrayal, and it is haunted by a giant octopus. The book was also responsible for introducing the Guernésiais word for octopus (*pieuvre*) into the French language. Hugo dedicated *Travailleurs de la mer* to the people of Guernsey. He later wrote that the lack of distraction on Guernsey enabled him to do as much work in a month here as he would get done in a year in Paris.

Visiting Hauteville House is an extraordinary experience. It is a work of art in its own right. Moreover, it is an insight into the mind of Victor Hugo. Walking through it is like coming face to face with the man himself; full of energy and ideas, brilliant, florid and off-the-scale egocentric. It's impossible not to be impressed.

THE CHALET, SARK – MERVYN PEAKE (1911–68)

Everyone knows there are no cars on Sark. What is less well known is that you cannot ride a bicycle down to the harbour, or kill a seagull, or take anything washed up on the beach as it belongs by right to the Seigneur.

Sark is the nearest thing to a feudal state we have in Europe. There is no income tax, and property passes strictly down the male line. Except that Sark isn't quite in Europe. It isn't part of Britain either but rather owes its loyalty directly to whoever is sitting on the English throne. The Seigneur pays a small amount of money every year to the Crown and undertakes to organise defences so that the island doesn't fall into the hands of the wicked French.

Sark is idiosyncratic to put it mildly, and the same might be said of Mervyn Peake, one of the most imaginative writers in the English language but also a superb illustrator. Peake came to Sark for the first time in 1933. He was 22 and arrived to join an artists' colony, painting in a building that is still known as The Gallery at the end of The Avenue, Sark's only named street. When the colony broke up in 1936, Peake left but he returned for a holiday in 1938 with his new wife. He was drawn back again after the Second World War, once the last of the Wehrmacht had left. The Dame of Sark, daughter of the Seigneur, had kept the French out but unfortunately been unable to defend her island against the wicked Germans.

Photo courtesy of Richard Drewe

Photo: Adrian Mourby

From 1946 to 1950 Peake worked on Sark at his *Gormenghast* trilogy of novels and *Mr Pye*, a fantasy novel about a pious man, newly arrived on Sark, who sprouts angel wings. *Mr Pye* was printed in 1953 with Peake's own illustrations three years after he, his wife and children had moved back to London. It was a publishing oddity that became mainstream when adapted in four episodes for television in 1985. The Mr Pye series was of course shot on Sark, making some of the island's idiosyncrasies famous around the world.

I arrived on Sark after a journey that involved flying from Southampton airport to Guernsey, staying there overnight and then getting the early-morning ferry that takes tourists, supplies and the British newspapers on the 45-minute crossing to Sark.

As soon as you arrive at the tiny port, it is obvious that Sark is a very different world. Transportation is by horse and cart, or by tractor – which some Sarkese still dislike, likening them to armoured tanks. Otherwise you go by foot – or hire a bike. This means that Sark's one street is congested each time a boat disgorges tourists. Bikes, horses, tractors and pedestrians congregate at the top of the harbour hill until dispersed in their various directions.

I took a pony and trap to La Sablonnerie, one of the island's two hotels, which is on Little Sark. Here, as on so much of Sark, you step into a time warp because the owner offers no Wi-fi, no television, not even any radio.

Little Sark is the smaller of the two granite islands that comprise the Isle of Sark. They are attached to each other by a narrow causeway 250 feet above sea-level. Peake described the topography as 'wasp-waisted'. A steep single track, known as La Coupée, runs over this narrow isthmus. Peake's Mr Pye finally escapes his persecutors here, when the angelic wings that have sprouted on his back bear him into the sky, and his horse and buggy crash into the sea. La Coupée is immediately recognisable to those who have read the book. Before the Second World War there wasn't even a handrail here, which meant that school children from Little Sark were advised on windy days to cross on their hands and knees to avoid being blown away.

I settled happily in to La Sablonnerie, which is a sequence of comfortably converted farm buildings round a lush garden and with no locks on the bedroom doors. After the initial unease I accepted this. Why would there be locks? Any thief who raided your room would have to queue up for the boat to Guernsey with everyone else, making it very easy for Sark's one constable to finger his collar.

On my second day I set out in search of Mervyn Peake's Sark. This meant cadging a lift with the hotel's horse and carriage on its way to the harbour. The hotel owner explained to the toothless young driver that he was to drop me at Clos des Vins.

'That's not Clos des Vins,' replied the coachman. 'That's Mervyn Peake's house.'

It took 25 minutes to get there, partly because all passengers have to get down at La Coupée and walk across and then get back on board on the other side of this terrifying precipice. I could probably have walked the whole distance in the same time, but it's a rare pleasure to travel by horse and carriage these days.

We stopped outside Clos des Vins, which was known as *Le Chalet* in Peake's time. It sits behind a white gate and is whitewashed, with large picture windows and a huge garden. I'd been told the owner was in France, but by phone to La Sablonnerie she'd confirmed that she was happy for me to look through the windows. Here I saw big empty rooms awaiting redecoration but it was the exterior that threw me.

The old mullioned windows were gone. The rough stone walls had been plastered smooth. One door had become a small window and a wraparound sun lounge had replaced the veranda. In short the place had been modernised beyond recognition. Nothing at Clos des Vins resembled the Gothic world of *Gormenghast* or even the Sark of *Mr Pye*. I suppose in my literary travels I was fortunate never to have encountered such a drastic makeover before.

In the afternoon I hired a bike and cycled up past La Seigneurie to Port du Moulin where there is a hidden shore carved out by the sea. Here the idealistic Mr Pye arranges for an invalid member of his flock to be lowered down to a prayer meeting during his beach festivity. Unfortunately she is left hanging in mid-air when everyone flees as the stinking carcass of a dead whale washes ashore.

You could see how the location would have inspired such an incident in the book. Later I found that a whale carcass did indeed wash up on Sark during Peake's time. When 'a large object on the shore' was reported to the Dame of Sark, she asserted her seigneurial right before discovering what it was she had just appropriated. The crafty constable had made sure the responsibility to dispose of the whale was now hers.

That evening I cycled back as far as La Coupée (you're not allowed to cross it by bicycle either) then walked the rest of the way to dinner, remembering Mr Pye's apotheosis. I concluded that while the house where Mervyn Peake lived and worked could tell me nothing, the island itself spoke volumes.

PARIS

BOULEVARD HAUSSMANN – MARCEL PROUST (1871–1922)

Marcel Proust lived most of his childhood and early adulthood in Boulevard Malesherbes, a three-minute walk from L'église de la Madeleine. Gabriel Fauré was the church's resident organist at this time and Fauré's first violin sonata, written when Proust was just four years old, is thought by some to be the inspiration for the 'little phrase' that infiltrates Swann's mind in the first volume of À *la recherche du temps perdu*.

These days there's a Bowen shoe shop on the ground floor of this identikit Baron Haussmann apartment block. My wife looked inside while I took some photos and tried to get a feel for this area which Proust called 'one of the ugliest parts of town'. The writer loved his parents dearly, but clearly wished they had not chosen to raise him in this upwardly-mobile arrondissement. Proust's spiritual home was Faubourg St Germain where France's superannuated aristocrats were sitting out their decline in grand townhouses, or *hôtels particuliers*.

In 1905, after the death of both his parents, the 34-year-old Proust moved not to his beloved St Germain but no distance at all to an apartment that had belonged to his maternal uncle. Because his adored mother had taken him to visit the apartment, Proust claimed that it exercised 'a tender and melancholy attraction'. Here on the second floor

of 102 Boulevard Haussman the author lived from 1906 to 1919, penning his seven-volume masterwork and growing increasingly eccentric as he wrote through the night and slept through the day in his cork-lined bedroom.

It's a seven-minute walk between the two apartments – and an interesting one too because you pass the *Chapelle expiatoire* dedicated to Louis XVI and Marie Antoinette. The king's body was initially interred here in this former cemetery with his guillotined head at his feet.

Arriving on Boulevard Haussmann we immediately noticed No. 102 across the road because it is now a prominent bank. In 1919 Proust's aunt sold the building to the banker René Varin-Bernier and her dispossessed nephew had to leave. The name Banque R. Varin-Bernier et Cie. is still inscribed on the cornice above the entrance, although a modern plastic sign confirms that it now trades as *Bank CIC*. A stone plaque on one of the pillars supporting the cornice announces that Marcel Proust 'habita cet immeuble de 1907 à 1919'. We both found it odd to think of him working away for twelve years at one of the greatest novels of the twentieth century above what is now the CIC Bank.

Towards the end of his eccentric – to put it mildly – life, Proust ventured out only at night. He once met James Joyce when the two men shared a cab, but Joyce recorded that they said very little to each other because he was tired and on his way to bed. 'Of course the situation was impossible,' wrote Joyce. 'Proust's day was just beginning. Mine was at an end.' On another occasion Proust rushed to the Louvre to check on a picture he wished to write about and was surprised to find the gallery was not open at midnight.

Fortunately our personal *recherche* for Proust was more successful at the Musée Carnavalet in Marais, just north of Notre-Dame. This museum was Baron Haussmann's idea. I'm sure the irony wasn't lost on him that having destroyed much of old Paris for the grandiose ambitions of Emperor Napoleon III, he created a museum to celebrate its lost history.

The museum contains the shoes of Marie-Antoinette and a ring made of her hair. There's also a document that Robespierre had not finished signing when he was dragged away under arrest, as well as Napoleon's favourite toiletry case, Émile Zola's gold watch and the cradle in which Napoleon III's son was rocked. There are also a number of paintings of busy nineteenth-century Paris that could be illustrations for *À la recherche du temps perdu*. But best of all is a recreation of Proust's bedroom, with his brass bedstead and furniture brought from various apartments in which he lived. There's a chaise and armchair, two small tables and a desk. I was very pleased to see the original cork wall tiles that lined his apartment at 102 Boulevard Haussmann. Proust could not bear distraction, so he worked with the windows closed and sound-proofed his room with these rectangular tiles.

Not surprisingly, by the end of his life the lack of sunshine and an abundance of cigarettes had taken its toll of an already delicate constitution. Céleste Albaret, Proust's servant, recorded taking him a croissant and having to push aside the heavy curtain that kept his door draught-proof: 'The smoke was so thick you could have cut it with a knife … All I could see of M. Proust was a white shirt under a thick sweater, and the upper part of his body propped against two pillows.'

She added that she couldn't actually make out Proust's visage at all in the fug and gloom: 'I bowed toward the invisible face and put the saucer with the croissant down on the tray. He gave a wave of the hand, presumably to thank me, but didn't say a word.'

Proust began and completed most of *À la recherche du temps perdu* in a smoky version of this room. In 1919 when the building was sold, after a brief stay with an actress friend (whose neighbours he could hear making love), Proust ended up at 44 Rue Hamelin with Céleste Albaret and her husband. Today this building near what is now Place Marlene Dietrich is the three-star Hotel Élysée Union and a plaque on its facade reads: 'Marcel Proust se réfugie 44 Rue Hamelin, où il meurt le 18 novembre 1922'.

Poor Proust. He dreamed of the *hôtels particuliers* of Faubourg St Germain but ended his days in what is now a commercial hotel – and a three-star one at that!

FOUQUET'S, AVENUE DES CHAMPS-ÉLYSÉES – JAMES JOYCE (1882–1941)

Ernest Hemingway once wrote of walking penniless through Paris with his wife Hadley and seeing James Joyce holding court in a warm, fine, brightly-lit restaurant. Given the location Hem describes, it was probably Fouquet's, but knowing Hemingway's ability to conjure up true events that never happened, it might easily have been any number of other restaurants. It might never have happened at all.

What is true is that James Joyce spent far more time in Paris than he ever did in Dublin. And that he wrote exclusively about the latter while living in the former.

Joyce first visited Paris in 1902 as a hungry student lodging in the Latin Quarter, wondering if he should become a doctor, and reading all day in the National Library. He returned in 1920 aged 38 at the invitation of expatriate American poet Ezra Pound. Joyce and his common-law wife Nora Barnacle, along with their two children, ended up living in Paris for the next twenty years. Here he worked on *Finnegans Wake* and here Sylvia Beach published *Ulysses* from her bookshop, Shakespeare and Company, at 12 Rue de l'Odéon.

Finding James Joyce's Paris is not like looking for Joyce's Dublin. Books have been devoted to the locations that Joyce recreated on paper from his memories of Dublin – and many of the sites still look as he knew them before his self-imposed exile. But Paris was never Joyce's and today it's hard to track down his ghost. We know that he spent sixteen years here wrestling with *Finnegans Wake* and living off grants of money from the wealthy English philanthropist, Harriet Shaw Weaver. We know that he saw his status as an avant-garde writer rise sky-high while he lived in Paris, even as his own eyesight deteriorated to near-blindness. By the time Joyce left Paris for Switzerland, after the Nazi invasion of France, he was unable to go out on his own. In his last weeks there he would stand on the Pont de l'Alma with his secretary, Paul Léon, unable to even make out the Seine flowing below.

In my sentimental imaginings of Joyce as an Irish émigré I thought of him frequenting the Left Bank cafés of Paris. Instead, as he grew solvent and even prosperous, he preferred to eat at Fouquet's restaurant at 99 Avenue des Champs-Élysées.

On one memorable Boxing Day in 1937 the Joyces dined at Fouquet's in the company of Samuel Beckett and Peggy Guggenheim. That evening was the beginning of a brief but very intense affair between Beckett and Guggenheim. Peggy had been invited to eat with Joyce and Nora, as well as Joyce's son Giorgio and his wife Helen, a friend of Peggy's from New York. There's no record of what Joyce ordered that evening at Fouquet's, although he often just chewed on raw garlic and drank his favourite wine, Fendant de Sion, while others ate. Whether this was to save money or calories I don't know, but his correspondence with Nora suggests he loved food.

Photo: Erwmat

Beckett, a guest of the Joyces that evening, was 31 years old to Joyce's 55. Peggy was 39. She had met the handsome Irishman on a couple of occasions before, and after the dinner at Fouquet's they went for drinks to Giorgio and Helen's flat. Later Beckett offered to escort Peggy home, and the couple ended up spending not just that night but the whole of the following day in bed together, having sex and drinking champagne. The affair resumed shortly afterwards when Peggy was caretaking a friend's home in Montparnasse and Beckett stayed with her for a week. Then it petered out.

Beckett dined with Joyce again on 4 January 1938. A few days later Beckett was stabbed in the street by a pimp named Prudent and taken to hospital unconscious. Joyce was one of the first visitors to the hospital. At his insistence, and expense, Beckett was moved to a private room and received the best medical care.

These expatriates of Gertrude Stein's Lost Generation lived ordinary creative lives, devoting hours to the tasks of writing and worrying about paying bills, but what we remember when we think of Paris in the 20s and 30s is the bravado, the bad behaviour and the stories they told about each other. I particularly like Hemingway's claim that Joyce would enjoy provoking younger, more agile men in bars and then hide behind his athletic friend and yell, 'Deal with him, Hemingway, deal with him!!!'

Sitting in Fouquet's today on the corner of the Champs-Élysées and Avenue George V, it's clear that the restaurant with its distinctive red canopy and wood-panelled walls has gone some way upmarket since the days when Joyce downed his bottles of Fendant de Sion. The interior is full of photos of French movie stars because the Champs-Élysées is where many films are premiered in France, and at Fouquet's those who triumph in Cannes are treated to the 'meal of the winners'.

The restaurant, with its tables screened from the road by low green hedges, serves typical French brasserie food including *les escargots gros* and *foie gras de Fouquet*. There are some extravagant puddings too, like *dessert haute couture de Mayu Asada*, named after the Japanese movie star. Dining at Fouquet's is now a symbol of luxury and wealth in itself. Many of its midweek clientele are refreshing themselves after an intense morning's shopping at the enormous Louis Vuitton flagship store across the road. It's a world away from James Joyce, but I still found it easy to imagine Hemingway and Hadley walking past and gazing hungrily in.

Assuming that ever happened, of course.

HÔTEL LANCASTER – ERICH MARIA REMARQUE (1898–1970)

German novelist Erich Maria Remarque lived a dramatic life. Wounded and invalided out of the First World War, he penned *Im Westen nichts Neues* (*All Quiet on the Western Front*) in the 1920s while writing copy for a tyre manufacturer and working as a librarian and journalist. It took him two years to find a publisher for his anti-war novel, but the book's success in 1929 – and its Oscar-winning screen adaptation a year later – made him a literary star. The novel also made him enemies in the Nazi party. On 10 May 1933, the Nazi propaganda minister, Joseph Goebbels, had Remarque's pacifist works banned and publicly burned.

Living in Switzerland, safely beyond the reach of the Fatherland, Remarque led a double life, writing serious, compassionate books about the turmoil in Europe while using his earnings to date movie stars and collect paintings by Van Gogh and Cézanne.

In 1938, after the publication of *Drei Kameraden* (*Three Comrades*), a book that many believe inspired the film *The Deer Hunter*, he began an affair with actress Marlene Dietrich in Venice. She brought him with her when she returned to Paris. Marlene explained to her young daughter Maria that the novelist had told her at their first meeting that he was impotent and that she had replied, 'How wonderful!' La Dietrich had often confided to her daughter how she hated to do 'it' and how she much preferred talking and sleeping in bed.

In Paris Remarque was working on *Liebe deinen Nächsten* (published in English as *Flotsam*). The novel describes the stories of a number of characters who flee Germany at the time of National Socialism. Published in 1939, it too would be filmed in the US, as *So Ends Our Night* with Fredric March and Margaret Sullavan.

Marlene arranged for Remarque – whom she called 'Boni' – to stay with her at Hôtel Lancaster in Paris while the fourteen-year-old Maria was sent to stay nearby at the Hôtel Windsor.

The Lancaster, just off the Champs-Élysées, had been opened in 1924 by the Swiss hotelier Émile Wolf. It's a small hotel that has always prided itself on its discretion and is decorated with valuable antiques that Wolf and his staff found in Paris auction rooms. Many bedrooms are hung with original oil paintings by Boris Pastoukhoff, a Ukrainian artist who fled the Russian revolution in 1917 and financed his decade at the Lancaster by regularly presenting Mr Wolf with pictures in lieu of payment. Wolf always intended the Lancaster to be an *hôtel particulier* where guests took suites for an extended period of time – and only after being personally introduced. Marlene's husband had found her the hotel in

1937 and she lived there intermittently with various lovers until the outbreak of the Second World War.

Today the hotel doesn't look much different from how it appeared in 1938 when Remarque was installed in Room 401, although the levels of comfort have been discreetly enhanced and the carpets removed to reveal original 1920s parquet. I stayed in this room – now known as the Marlene Suite – soon after it was restored in 2012, and very comfortable it was too. Marlene's grandson, a Hollywood designer, had overseen the redesign using a lilac palette based on her favourite colour and brought in new furniture inspired by originals found in Marlene's New York apartment. The refurb had retained the original grand piano and there were lilies everywhere, in tribute to Marlene's habit of deluging the hotel with flowers.

In 1938 the suite was actually twice the size it is now. The section that was kept just for Marlene's clothes is now another whole suite. What interested me, however, was the bathroom. It's nowhere near as remarkable as the rest of 401, but it tells an unusual story.

One day in 1938 young Maria came to meet her mother and found two men with swastika armbands guarding the door to her mother's suite. The German foreign minister, Ulrich von Ribbentrop, had called on Marlene to ask her to return to Germany and become part of the Third Reich's film industry. She graciously declined and, after Ribbentrop left, Marlene instructed Maria to release Herr Remarque from the bathroom. Convinced the Nazis were after her lover because of his pacifist views and desertion of the Fatherland, Marlene had locked him in when Ribbentrop turned up. Remarque came out furious at his undignified imprisonment.

'Oh, my only love!' Dietrich insisted, 'I was only frightened for you! You know how they hate you!'

Photo: © Kate Tadman-Mourby

The high farce of this story does not find its way into any of Remarque's fiction.

When war broke out a year later, Marlene returned to the US with Remarque, who was travelling on a Panamanian passport. In 1940 the Wehrmacht marched into Paris and Mr Wolf's canny staff raised the owner's Swiss flag to make sure that no German soldiers were billeted on them. As a result, the Lancaster survived the Second World War without having any of its antiques or artwork plundered.

Remarque stayed in the US for some years, eventually marrying the actress Paulette Goddard when he finally realised Marlene would never be his. She admired his talent but didn't like how drunk he would get in the evenings. According to Maria, rather than being broken-hearted, Marlene was furious that Goddard would get all his priceless oil paintings.

Alcoholic or not, Remarque continued to be a hugely successful novelist during his time in America and then back in Switzerland, where he lived out the rest of his life after leaving the US in 1948. His last novel *Die Nacht von Lissabon* (*The Night in Lisbon*), published in 1962, sold nearly a million copies in Germany alone. He continued to correspond with Dietrich and a selection of their letters was published in 2003 as *Sag Mir, Dass Du Mich Liebst* (*Tell Me That You Love Me*) and later turned into a stage play.

These days the Lancaster is a popular choice for movie stars attending premieres on the Champs-Élysées. In 1967 Richard Burton and Elizabeth Taylor stayed in Room 701 for the French premiere of Zeffirelli's *The Taming of the Shrew*. Fortunately their suite was at the top of its own flight of stairs where, so the manager informed me, other guests could not hear their violent arguments.

LES DEUX MAGOTS, SAINT-GERMAIN-DES-PRÉS – JEAN-PAUL SARTRE (1905–80)

Les Deux Magots, taking its name from the two incongruous statues of Chinese merchants fixed so high above the clientele they almost touch the ceiling, is famous on the Paris tourist trail in a way that Café de Flore, the more overtly intellectual café next door, is not. Flore was considered right-wing in the 1930s, so when Jean-Paul Sartre arrived in Paris in 1937 to teach at Lycée Pasteur he gravitated towards Les Deux Magots. It had been a favourite of the previous generation of artists, the Hemingways and Picassos, who had enjoyed the real pleasure of Paris in the 20s.

Auguste Boulay, who had been running this café in a former fabric shop since 1914, wasn't political but his clientele – defining themselves in opposition to Charles Maurras, founder of the nationalist Action Française who had written his manifesto in Café de Flore – gave Les Deux Magots its reputation. It became left-wing by default. In 1933 Boulay had created its own (ever so slightly left-leaning) literary prize, which the café continues to fund.

In 1939 Sartre had to give up the comforts of Deux Magots' banquettes and marbled-topped tables when he was drafted into the French army. He was assigned to meteorological duties and denied a rifle because of his poor eyesight. In 1940 during the fall of France, Sartre was captured and spent nine months as a prisoner of war before being released in 1941 and returned to civilian life. He was given a position at Lycée Condorcet in Paris, replacing a Jewish teacher who had been forbidden to teach by the Vichy regime, and settled into Mistral on Rue Cels, one of his favourite Paris hotels.

Photo: Serge Melki

Deux Magots, two kilometres north along Rue de Rennes from Hôtel Mistral, was a good place for the pipe-smoking philosopher to walk to for the serious business of writing and tobacco. It was here that Sartre discussed resistance to the German occupation with his mistress Simone de Beauvoir and Albert Camus, concluding eventually that it was better to write than fight. In their case probably wisely too. It was also here that Sartre worked on his proposed tetralogy, *Les Chemins de la liberté* (*The Roads to Freedom*) while de Beauvoir (on a separate table) wrote her tale of immortality, *Tous les hommes sont mortels* (*All Men are Mortal*). Here too Sartre wrote a pen portrait of the typical Parisian waiter: 'He comes toward the patrons with a step a little too quick. He bends forward a little too eagerly, his eyes express an interest too solicitous for the order of the customer.'

I've been intimidated by waiters like that myself. I remember being caught looking at the brass plaques on the backs of the banquettes in Deux Magots a little too intensely by an overly-attentive waiter. I felt judged by the man in his crisp white shirt and black apron. He clearly had marked me down as 'tourist'. But if you put plaques with names like Sartre, de Beauvoir, and Hemingway on your seats, you're going to attract that kind of trade.

With the waiter hovering I was caught between ordering the *Petit Déjeuner Hemingway* and the *Petit Déjeuner JP Sartre*. Both cost 26 euros and you get two Danish pastries with the Sartre and fried egg and bacon with the Hem. Instead I just asked for a double espresso, sipped my coffee too quickly, and felt obliged to leave once the cup was empty. I've never managed the European way of renting a table by making your coffee last all morning. Perhaps that time-killing aspect is why French intellectuals smoked so much.

Ask any Parisian intellectual today – and there is no

shortage – and you will be told that just as the reputation of Sartre drew would-be philosophers and writers to Deux Magots in the 50s and 60s, so all the tourists who followed in their wake have since driven the thinkers away. Flore, having been shunned for its 1930s anti-Semitism and the legacy of Charles Maurras, is now where the intelligent coffee-drinker goes to occupy his or her table.

Deux Magots is now run by Catherine Mathivat, the great-great granddaughter of Auguste Boulay. Through brass signs and menu choices she has ensured that it has cornered the market as the philosophers' café on the Left Bank as far as tourists are concerned. Actually after the Second World War de Beauvoir and Sartre decamped to the bar of the Pont-Royal Hotel on Rue du Bac in the 7th arrondissement, having grown fed up of being gawped at by literary groupies. In 1949, by now a leading figure in French literature, Sartre was stung by the review for the third instalment of *Les Chemins de la liberté* and never completed the fourth. He retired to another arrondissement entirely, to lick his wounds, polish his glasses and garner award after award.

Some revisionists will tell you that during the war Sartre eschewed Les Deux Magots when it became too popular with officers from the Wehrmacht. I've even read that during the harsh winter of 1943–4 the warm stove upstairs at Café de Flore caused Sartre to forget all about its right-wing reputation and decamp next door. But then Paris would not be Paris without some sharp disagreement between those who consider themselves intellectuals.

BERLIN

CHAUSSEESTRASSE – BERTOLT BRECHT (1898–1956)

The old Prussian capital of Berlin is associated with many German writers – Hegel, Theodor Fontane and Christa Wolf – as well as 1920s émigrés like Vladimir Nabokov and the young English sybarites Auden and Isherwood, who came seeking something exciting in Weimar Berlin (and definitely found it). But Bertolt Brecht is perhaps the writer most closely linked to the capital because of the plays he wrote and directed here until 1933 and the work that followed when Brecht and his wife Helene Weigel returned to a divided Berlin in 1947 after the Second World War.

For all that his name is virtually synonymous with the Berliner Ensemble, Brecht was not born in this tragic city. Eugen Berthold Friedrich Brecht (known as Eugen by his family) was a Swabian from Augsburg who came to Berlin in the 1920s to found a theatre company with the playwright Arnolt Bronnen. He actually changed his name to Bertolt so it would rhyme with Arnolt on the theatre billing.

From his earliest works for stage, Brecht was successful. In 1924 while still in his mid-20s he was awarded the prestigious Kleist Prize for unestablished writers. Brecht went on to pen a prodigious number of dramas, including *Leben Eduards des Zweiten von England* (*The Life of Edward II of England*, 1924), *Die Dreigroschenoper* (*The Threepenny Opera*, 1928) and *Die Mutter* (*The Mother*, 1930–32). The times were turning against him, however, and by the time Adolf Hitler was elected Chancellor in 1933, Brecht, like Christopher Isherwood, was packing his bags.

Brecht and his wife fled first to Scandinavia and then to the USSR before ending up in the US. In 1947 they returned, seeking refuge in the Russian-controlled Mitte area of Berlin, later to become part of the Communist GDR. Given his left-wing political views, Brecht was not welcome in embattled West Berlin and his hopes of neutral Vienna and Austrian citizenship had been thwarted. So he took up residence in East Berlin and was soon lauded as the GDR's artistic figurehead. Here he established the Berliner Ensemble for whom he continued to write plays until his death.

I was in Berlin in 2013 to write about the possibility that the Ensemble might be losing their home at the Theater am Schiffbauerdamm. Rumours that this shrine to Brechtian stagecraft was going to be turned into luxury apartments proved to be unfounded and so, without a story, I went for lunch at Ganymed, an excellent nearby brasserie where the Stasi used to keep microphones in the flower arrangements. Then I set off to see if I could visit Brecht's apartment on Chausseestrasse. Brecht and Weigel moved into this three-storey block in 1953, taking two flats on different floors (their model of domestic harmony) with use of the ground-floor kitchen.

It was just a ten-minute walk north of Brecht's theatre on the River Spree up a broad, intermittently suburban street (though Brecht always drove). Just before reaching No. 125 you pass a lane down to the Dorotheenstädtischer cemetery where Hegel, Marcuse, Günter Grass and Christa Wolf are buried. There is also a memorial to those members of the 20 July plot against Adolf Hitler, who were executed nearby. The back of the Brechthaus overlooks this cemetery. It is a heavy, solid-looking building and open to the public for

guided tours. One of the two women on reception said she would be showing people round in German in twenty minutes if I did not mind a tour in Brecht's own language. Even if my German is limited to the odd snatch of poetry and ordering *Wurst mit Senf,* how could I demur? So I paid my 5 euros to save a place and went for a coffee at the Kellerrestaurant im Brecht-Haus downstairs to read up about the apartment, which is now officially the Brecht-Weigel Memorial. In Chausseestrasse Brecht worked on his last plays, *Turandot* (1954), *Don Juan* (1952–4) and *Pauken und Trompeten* (*Trumpets and Drums,* 1955). He died of a heart attack in his flat in 1956. Helene stayed on, creating the Brecht archive and keeping the flame burning. She died in 1971, and in 1978 this building became a memorial to both of them.

Arriving back on the first floor, our small group found a useful timeline on Brecht's life in the first room and then a sequence of uncluttered living spaces, rather as I had expected of a man with Brecht's clarity and convictions. Not for him the commercial impedimenta of a bourgeois existence. There were over 4,000 books, though – with a surprising number of crime thrillers – and a few East Asian artefacts, including three Japanese Noh masks on the wall.

As I followed our guide round, there seemed to be a writing desk with a typewriter in almost every room. Our tall, rather sad lady told us that Brecht wanted to be able to write things down as soon as they came into his mind. To me it was quite an insight into the man that he'd do so on a typewriter rather than in a notebook. I found myself thinking of Brecht the text machine.

One of the rear rooms had large side windows overlooking the cemetery where Brecht and Weigel are now buried. The guide told us that the fact that Hegel – whose Dialectics he admired – was interred there had appealed to Brecht when taking this apartment.

Then we trooped downstairs to the kitchen with its state-of-the-art GDR refrigerator installed after Brecht's death. I don't normally pay much attention to authorial kitchens. Unless the owner of the house was a keen cook, the kitchen gives away very little autobiographically. I would have imagined the functional Mr Brecht with a can opener, a shelf of tins and some ashtrays. This was a very well-equipped kitchen, however, with a stove with four gas burners and an old-fashioned dresser that must have been here before the Second World War. But then as our lady reminded me in an English aside, Helene Weigel was not just an accomplished actress and artistic collaborator, she loved cooking. Members of the Berliner Ensemble praised her dishes, particularly the crispy deep-fried chicken, and a sketch by Marc Chagall shows the playwright reclining while Weigel rushes over to provide him with cakes.

I think that was my first-ever authorial insight in a kitchen.

NOLLENDORFSTRASSE – CHRISTOPHER ISHERWOOD (1904–86)

When Christopher Isherwood moved to Berlin at the end of 1929, the 25-year-old British writer couldn't settle. He camped out in several different apartments before finally plumping for an address that was to have a big impact on his literary output. Nollendorfstrasse 17 was a tall, double-fronted terraced house in the city's theatrical Schöneberg district and part of its unofficial gay quarter. Here Christopher became (in his own words) 'a camera'.

Photo: © Kate Tadman-Mourby

I went on an Isherwood hunt one Saturday morning while staying at Berlin's old Adlon Hotel, but I was not optimistic. By the end of the Second World War nowhere had had so many bombs rain down upon it as Berlin. I didn't expect to find much of Isherwood in the city he said goodbye to in 1933 and turned into a novella in 1939. *Goodbye to Berlin* in turn inspired a play, *I Am a Camera* (1951), which inspired a film of the same name (1955) and a musical called *Cabaret* (1966), which became a film (1972) that brought Liza Minnelli an Oscar for her career-best performance as Sally Bowles.

Sally was based on Jean Ross, whom Isherwood met when she moved into Nollendorfstrasse 17 in 1931. She was twenty with a long aristocratic nose, and at the time was on what today we would call her gap year. Although Jean boasted childishly of her many lovers and sang a little, she had a serious side. She was a member of the Communist party and soon after leaving Berlin in 1932 married the celebrated left-wing British journalist Claud Cockburn.

When Isherwood came to fictionalise his time in Berlin he gave her the name Sally Bowles, inspired by his meeting with the handsome young American composer Paul Bowles. 'I liked the sound of it and also the looks of its owner,' he later confided.

It's ironic that the film *Cabaret* – a glamorous work far removed from Christopher Isherwood's experience of 1930s Germany – has, for many of us, come to define Berlin during Hitler's rise to power. With a head full of its divinely decadent images, I set off on my search for 'Issyvoo', walking south through Berlin's Tiergarten. This was new territory for me; I've been visiting East Berlin since the Wall came down in 1989 but Isherwood's home was in what would become the West after 1945. Living on a modest private income, Isherwood arrived at Nollendorfstrasse after sharing a leaking attic apartment in Kreuzberg with one of his young proletarian lovers – and the young man's family – and a room next to the Magnus Hirschfeld Institute for Sexual Science.

'He liked to imagine himself as one of those mysterious wanderers who penetrate the depths of a foreign land,' Isherwood wrote in *Christopher and His Kind*, '... and die in unknown graves, envied by their stay-at-home compatriots.'

It wasn't hard to locate the house where in December 1930 Christopher Isherwood became a lodger of Fräulein Meta Thurau. She named him 'Herr Issyvoo' and inspired the character of Fräulein Schröder, a respectable hausfrau forced to take in lodgers after the economic disaster of the Weimar Republic. In *Goodbye to Berlin* poverty has turned Fräulein Schröder into a Jew-hating supporter of Hitler.

Nollendorfstrasse today is tree-lined and prosperously residential. The scars of war are evident only when you notice buildings like the house next door to No. 17, which was blown up and replaced in the 1950s by something inappropriate and blandly concrete. Remarkably, however, the house where Christopher met his future Sally Bowles still stands. It's surprisingly grand, with an ochre facade, two front doors and five floors rising up above a basement. Three of those floors have rooms with balconies overlooking the street and in one of these rooms Isherwood gave English lessons to supplement his income.

These days the basement of No. 17 is a shop selling second-hand and rare books – including the odd edition of *Goodbye to Berlin* – while the rest of the house is residential. There is a plaque next to the very ornate wood-and-glass front door informing us that Christopher Isherwood lived here 'Von Marz 1929 Bis Jan/Feb 1933' which is unfortunately wrong. Isherwood arrived in Berlin in the March of 1929 to visit his friend W.H. Auden, leaving and returning three times in that year before finally deciding in November to stay and finding a home in Nollendorfstrasse.

Today across the street there's a private cocktail bar called Stagger Lee with red wallpaper and old leather armchairs. Two blocks north on Eisenacher Strasse I found a 1920s-style café with musical performances every Wednesday night that has adopted the name Sally Bowles. The shelves of spirits are lit with red lights, recreating something of the Isherwood world without resorting to pastiche.

Nollendorfstrasse is still part of the Berlin gay scene, however. There are shops selling leather and rubber outfits, a large LGBT bookshop, and a café called Romeo & Romeo.

In Herr Issyvoo's day the Eldorado Club, famed for its drag artistes, was nearby on the corner of Motzstrasse. Customers could purchase tokens for dances with beautiful young people, with the added frisson that you could not always tell which gender you were embracing. Otto Dix famously painted its patrons – women with Eton-cropped hair and monocles, men in women's clothing – sybarites whose faces would become the epitome of Weimar decadence. Today, however, a modern housing block with a supermarket on its ground floor occupies the site of the Eldorado, which was closed by the Nazis in 1933 and then destroyed by Allied bombing. This is the nearest we can authentically get to Isherwood's Kit Kat Club. A sign over the supermarket door reads 'Speisekammer im Eldorado' (Pantry in the Eldorado). The divinely decadent is now given over to the fruit and veg.

As you enter, a few photos show how the nightclub looked in the days of Dix and Isherwood: narrow but crammed with white table cloths, mismatched chandeliers, dark corners and gilded ceilings.

By the time Isherwood left Berlin, boy bars like the Cosy Corner on Zossener Strasse that he so enjoyed were being raided and shut down by Hitler's Brownshirts. In May 1933 Isherwood said goodbye to Germany for good in the company of his lover Heinz Neddermeyer. Heinz was later apprehended and forced into the German army while Isherwood sat out much of the war in America.

Unusually for a writer, Christopher Isherwood did return to the rooms that had inspired him. On a visit in 1952 he was saddened by the sight of 'smashed buildings along that familiar street'. In those days of East/West tension the surviving facades were still pitted by shrapnel. What a shame he never saw Berlin reunited and the city he loved for all its naughtiness restored to how it is today.

I genuinely could imagine Isherwood and his Sally walking along this tree-lined street, aspiring to be divinely decadent.

NEW YORK & NEW ORLEANS

THE BUCKINGHAM HOTEL, NEW YORK – DAMON RUNYON (1880–1946)

Damon Runyon is one of those writers so deeply associated with the city in which he wrote that he bequeathed New York an adjective: Runyonesque.

It helped that he lived the life he wrote about. Runyon was the archetype of the tough, hard-nosed street reporter who fraternised with gangsters, bookmakers and sportsmen. Al Capone was a friend, so was the boxer Jack Dempsey and the baseball player Babe Ruth.

He smoked and drank coffee continuously and when he wasn't in his apartment, he was usually making notes in Lindy's Deli – when he wasn't at the Stork Club. Runyon was hardly ever home, leading his first wife, Ellen, to claim that if he died and she went to his funeral she doubted she would recognise any of the other mourners.

Damon Runyon chronicled New York in the 1920s, 30s and early 40s through his journalism and short stories. In tales like *The Idyll of Miss Sarah Brown*, *Blood Pressure* and *Pick the Winner*, his New Yorkers spoke in an idiosyncratic mix of formality and slang that can still be found widely emulated from the gunmen in *Kiss Me Kate*, to Woody Allen's *Bullets Over Broadway*, and even *The Sopranos*. They went by the most marvellous names: Nicely-Nicely Johnson, Benny Southstreet, Good Time Charley, Dave the Dude and Harry

the Horse. Sixteen Runyon stories were turned into films, and his books are still popular today.

For most people, however, the Runyonesque magnum opus is *Guys and Dolls*, a musical that was pulled together after his death from three of his short stories written in the 1930s. Sadly Runyon was long gone before it opened in 1950 on Broadway, the winding showbiz street that he loved – and over which his ashes had already been scattered by Captain Eddie Rickenbacker. It's no surprise that the scattering of anything from a biplane weaving between Manhattan's skyscrapers was highly illegal, or that Rickenbacker, America's most successful First World War fighter ace, was another of Runyon's many male friends.

Damon Runyon lived and wrote with such brio that I had my doubts that I would find anything sufficiently Runyonesque when I visited New York in the winter of 2014. I went looking for Lindy's first. Lindy's was the Broadway deli where – allegedly – the line 'Waiter, there's a fly in my soup' received its first witty riposte. Lindy's was opened by Leo Lindermann and his wife Clara in 1921. The Jewish Mafia don Arnold Rothstein referred to it as his 'office' and conducted business there surrounded by bodyguards. The comedian Milton Berle always ate dinner at Lindy's, and Runyon, long-time baseball correspondent for Hearst newspapers, was another regular, smoking, sipping coffee and scribbling in a notebook when he wasn't talking the talk. Lindy's, which features in *Guys and Dolls* as 'Mindy's', was also famous for its cheesecake.

There is a new Lindy's in Manhattan just one block south of Broadway on 7th Avenue. It advertises its 'World Famous' Cheesecake, serves you in old-fashioned booths and uses an Art Deco typeface on the menus, but it's a new enterprise by the Riese Organization which took over the trademark in 1979. The original Lindy's was half a mile away at 1626 Broadway, between 49th and 50th Streets. It closed in 1957 and became a steakhouse, but I was keen to see the site anyway. So I followed the street numbers down Broadway only to find a big, modern mixed-use block which, since 1992, contains Caroline's, a top New York comedy club. It's nice to know that humour continues at this address and evidently the 280-seat performance space received an architectural award, but it was hardly Runyonesque.

So I walked the short distance to the Stork Club at 3 East 53rd Street. From what I had read of Damon Runyon's daily life in New York, he followed a triangular route in the canyons of skyscrapers just south of Central Park. The Stork was established on West 58th Street in 1929 by Sherman Billingsley, an Oklahoma bootlegger. After it was raided by agents of the Prohibition it moved twice, ending up on East 53rd Street, just east of 5th Avenue, in 1934.

The 5th Avenue Stork Club wasn't big. It consisted of a dining room and bar and an oval 'Cub Room' which Billingsley built on for card games. There were no windows in the Cub Room, just wood-panelled walls hung with portraits of women, and a lot of smoke. On the door was a *maître d'* known as Saint Peter who determined who was allowed to enter. Here Damon Runyon wrote, and added to the carcinogenic fug. In 1942 Hemingway claimed he was able to cash his $100,000 cheque for the film rights to *For Whom the Bell Tolls* at the club and thereby settle his bar bill, but that's probably as true as most Hemingway stories.

In 1947, when *Cosmopolitan* published the last magazine article written by Damon Runyon, it was about the Stork Club, which he likened to London's Mermaid Tavern in the days of Jonson and Marlowe: 'A Mermaid Tavern complete with debutantes.'

When I found 3 East 53rd Street, nothing was there; nothing in the sense that after the club closed in 1965 it was demolished and an urban 'pocket' park was constructed by Bill Paley, chief executive of CBS, whose wife was adored by Truman Capote. Paley Park is a tranquil ivy-clad spot with a twenty-foot waterfall across its back wall that subtly drowns out the sound of traffic. It was difficult to believe that so much life and braggadocio once went on in this very small space.

Having struck out twice, I walked north to 101 West 57th Street with little optimism. This address had belonged to the Buckingham Hotel, where Runyon lived until his death in 1946. A favourite story he told against himself was about going out one morning and leaving a young lady still in his bed, and being hailed by a friend who pointed out that Runyon was not wearing a hat. Damon Runyon was known for his hats. So he returned to the Buckingham only to find his lady friend 'playing house' with the boxing champion Primo Carnera. Asked what a gentleman does when he finds his beloved in the arms of such a boxer, Runyon replied: 'It's all in the hat – you put it on and leave in a hurry.'

I knew the Buckingham had closed a few years earlier, so I expected to find the scene of this anecdote now a Starbucks or parking lot, but in fact as I turned the corner from 6th Avenue, there was the hotel where Ignaz Paderewski, Georgia O'Keeffe and Marc Chagall had at various times been Runyon's neighbours. It's now called The Quin (as in Quintessential New York), and had recently opened after a major refurbishment to create a twenty-first-century interior. But on the outside in all its brick verticality it is still 1929, the year in which the Buckingham opened. I could easily see Damon Runyon hurrying through those revolving doors in search of his hat, and coming back out even faster.

THE ALGONQUIN HOTEL, NEW YORK – DOROTHY PARKER (1893–1967)

The Algonquin Hotel opened in 1902. Its location on West 44th Street was close to many New York theatres. This was originally intended as a residential hotel – like the Chelsea – but the proprietors soon discovered that rooms let commercially at $2 a night were more profitable. In the 1920s the hotel became linked with a coterie of witty and acerbic writers, including Alexander Woollcott, George S. Kaufman, Robert Benchley and Robert E. Sherwood. But it will always be associated for most of us with Dorothy Rothschild Parker. Mrs Parker was one of the youngest members of the waspish Round Table who lunched at the 'Gonk' as often as six days a week for nearly ten years in the 1920s. She was also one of the few women in the group which awarded itself various nicknames over the years, including 'the Vicious Circle'.

The Circle started off dining in the hotel's Pergola Room (now called the Oak Room). When it grew too large and rowdy, the owner-manager, Frank Case, moved them into his main dining room, the Rose Room, seating them at a round table which later gave its name to the Round Table Restaurant.

When she was first invited along as drama critic of *Vanity Fair*, Dorothy Parker was 25 and on the verge of becoming famous both as a writer and as the prototype for other people's wise-cracking female characters. Philip Barry created a 'Dottie' clone in *Hotel Universe* (1932), as did George Oppenheimer in *Here Today* (1932), and George S. Kaufman in *Merrily We Roll Along* (1934). Kaufman's representation of a heavy-drinking Mrs Parker precipitated a breach between Dottie and her former Round Table compatriot. She got a

revenge of sorts, however, outstripping him in fame, with Kaufman admitting eventually: 'Everything I've ever said will be credited to Dorothy Parker.'

Mrs Parker also lived at the Algonquin from time to time. In 1924 after she split – for the second time – from her husband, the handsome WASP stockbroker Eddie Pond Parker, Dorothy moved temporarily into a furnished suite on the second floor. She lived there again after the Vicious Circle disbanded in 1929, and in 1932 she attempted suicide in her room at the Algonquin. (Mrs Parker attempted suicide three times. Being brittle, female and funny can exact a toll.)

I wasn't sure that the Algonquin existed any more, but in 2012 I found out that it was undergoing a major refurbishment, and arranged to be in New York when the press were invited round. The new Algonquin was slated to have over twenty new suites named after its famous lunchers. There would be a James Thurber Suite and a John Barrymore Suite, aptly just above the Blue Bar (it was Barrymore who in 1933 convinced Frank Case to put blue gels over the lighting in the bar because he believed they improved one's appearance). There was also going to be a Dorothy Parker Suite, although no one was sure if it would be one of the actual rooms in which she lived – and attempted to die. Up on the tenth floor where Frank Case and his wife raised two children in Suite 1010, a new Noël Coward Suite would be named after one of the occasional outsiders to grace the Algonquin's Round Table.

My interest was not in the bedrooms, however, but in the Round Table Restaurant, where Mrs Parker probably thought up – and certainly delivered – some of her best one-liners. The Algonks loved charades, pranks and parlour games. One of these was called 'I can give you a sentence'. Given the word 'horticulture', Dorothy Parker famously riposted: 'You can lead a horticulture but you can't make her think.'

Much of what we think of as classic Dorothy Parker wit was written during her Algonquin days. Here she collaborated with playwright Elmer Rice to create *Close Harmony*, which opened on Broadway in 1924. Her first volume of verse, *Enough Rope*, came out in 1926 and the second, *Sunset Gun*, in 1928. She also wrote short stories, such as 'The Garter', which was published in *The New Yorker* in 1928, and 'Big Blonde', which won the O. Henry Award for best short story of 1929.

In 1934 Dorothy moved on to Hollywood with her second husband. She earned a fortune writing for the movies, but that was not the Mrs Parker I was looking for. I wanted the wisecracking Queen of Literary Manhattan.

So it was, in 2013, a month after the completion of an excruciatingly expensive refurbishment, that I went to lunch at the Algonquin. Tales of the nine-month building work sounded alarming. The old plumbing, which had been built into the walls as the hotel was constructed, had had to be dug out and replaced, pipe by pipe. But I was pleased to see that the Round Table Room was refurbished with dark wood panelling and studded leather dining chairs that recalled the early twentieth century without being too precise. Strict Art Deco lines had been kept for the Blue Bar but, alas, there was no large round table, nowhere where you could pull up your chair and try to be witty. Nevertheless there is a very good painting on display by the young New York artist Natalie Ascencios. Her 'Vicious Circle' shows Harold Ross in the foreground, reading *The New Yorker* with Alexander Woollcott leaning over his shoulder. Dorothy Parker sits, poised and brittle, to the left of the picture.

To eat I ordered Matilda's Crab Cakes (named after the hotel's cat, now in her third incarnation). It was John Barrymore who made the Algonquin cat an institution by renaming Frank Case's stray moggy 'Hamlet' in the 1930s. There have now been seven Algonquin Hamlets and three Matildas.

Lunch was very enjoyable but I came away with the feeling that if the Algonks were reincarnated today they'd eschew this room as too respectable, too attuned to modern sensibilities. These days NYC health regulations have banned Matilda from the dining areas.

There's no doubting the frisson of being in the very room where Dorothy drawled her witticisms. She was particularly hard on actresses, claiming that Katharine Hepburn 'runs the gamut of emotions from A to B' and that Marion Davies 'has two expressions: joy and indigestion'. Of Edith Evans she once claimed, 'Edith looks like something that would eat its young', but my favourite remains her view of the writer's profession: 'I hate writing, I love having written.' Like the very best wit, that contains so much truth.

HOTEL CHELSEA, NEW YORK – DYLAN THOMAS (1914–53)

For generations the Chelsea was New York's most glamorously notorious hotel. Dylan Thomas' death in 1953 from alcohol poisoning, pneumonia and what was referred to as 'a severe insult to the body' did a lot to cement its dubious reputation. Cheap rooms and 70 years of benign, scarily laissez-faire management by the Bard family made the Chelsea a magnet for generations of bohemians in the Big Apple.

The twelve-storey red brick city block was built in 1884 by Philip Hubert, an idealistic Anglo-French immigrant who hoped that at the Chelsea he could design a truly socialist building in which the rich and poor could live in harmony.

By 1905, however, this bold experiment on West 23rd Street had failed and the Chelsea was reinvented as a hotel. In its 102 years of life, right up until the Bard family were driven out of business in 2007, it proved irresistible to writers, artists and musicians. Frida Kahlo, Mark Rothko, Edith Piaf, Brendan Behan, Arthur C. Clarke and Leonard Cohen all stayed at the Chelsea. Arthur Miller lived here for six years in the 1960s after his break-up with Marilyn Monroe and claimed you could get high just by standing in the hotel lifts and inhaling the marijuana smoke. Jack Kerouac wrote sections of *On the Road* while staying at the Chelsea. A hotel legend runs that in March 1953 Kerouac met his friend Gore Vidal at the Chelsea, both intent on meeting up with the poet Dylan Thomas, newly arrived from Wales. Failing to find Thomas, the two men got very drunk and ended up spending a passionate night together, an event that Kerouac later recorded in a bowdlerised version in his 1958 novel *The Subterraneans*.

Dylan Thomas actually arrived in New York on 21 April of that year. He had promised to hand over his new play for voices, *Under Milk Wood*, on arrival but it was finished only on the day of the first performance three weeks later. Liz Reitell, an assistant at the Poetry Center on East 92nd Street where the work was being premiered, had to lock the hard-drinking Dylan in his room until it was completed. Liz was also Dylan's American girlfriend by this stage, but the poet was simultaneously writing desperate love letters to his wife Caitlin in Wales. Dylan Thomas' life was often a mess, but it was spinning wholly out of control at this time. One night he fell downstairs drunk and broke his arm, and when he and Liz went to see Arthur Miller's *The Crucible* at the Martin

Photo: Nancyannpg

Beck Theatre on West 45th Street he started jeering and swearing at the actors and was asked to leave.

Back in Wales that summer, Dylan found he couldn't work. He lost a version of *Under Milk Wood* that he was writing for the BBC in a Soho pub and fled once again to New York, where Liz took him back. Unfortunately he couldn't get the room he wanted at the Chelsea and he complained that in the small room he was given at the rear of the hotel, the cockroaches had teeth. This visit was even more erratic than the previous one. Despite Stravinsky wanting to work on an opera with him, and a lecture agent offering $1,000 a week if he'd go on the circuit, Dylan drank, argued with everyone and screamed in the night as terrors engulfed him. On 4 November he came back from his last drinking binge and announced to Liz that he had just drunk eighteen whiskeys. He then fell asleep and on 5 November muttered, 'After 39 years this is all I've done', before slipping into a coma. On 9 November he died in St Vincent's Hospital.

Today a brass plaque outside the Hotel Chelsea records that here 'Dylan Thomas laboured his last and sailed out to die'. It's a poetic way to put it. I visited the hotel after it had been sold to developers in 2007 and long before the refurbishment began to turn it into the flagship of the short-lived Chelsea Hotels Group. Its long pink and white awning still stretched into the street and inside there was a scattering of old armchairs across the tiled lobby. The walls above a small reception booth were almost obliterated with artwork, not all of it good. There was a large pink papier-mâché female figure hanging from the ceiling. Some of the cubbyholes behind reception were jammed full of uncollected mail for guests and residents, but many had already departed.

The lobby with its mismatched chairs and abandoned newspapers reminded me of a student common room from the 1960s, and not a very tidy one at that. I asked if I could have a look at the famous wrought-iron staircase that winds up the hotel's lightwell. Officially tours had to be booked but the man behind reception just shrugged. So off I went on my own. The staircase is a robust piece of nineteenth-century construction that matches the balconies on the outside of the hotel. Looking for Room 205 where Dylan drank his last, I found some graffiti etched into the badly-painted plaster that commemorated punk rocker Sid Vicious who murdered his girlfriend Nancy Spungen here in 1978. By then the building had slipped from notoriety to legendary squalor.

If the hotel ever reopens, it will of necessity present a cleaned-up version of its wild literary past. There aren't enough roaring boys out there these days to make a Chelsea Mark II profitable. But there are many other sights connected with Dylan that haven't changed. Liz Reitell recorded that for a few days after checking into the Chelsea in October 1953, Dylan had hardly drunk and enjoyed going for walks with her around the various villages of New York. He liked Patchin Place, a gated cul de sac near Washington Square Park where he used to visit the poet e e cummings. Dylan also liked St Luke in the Fields, a small church built on Hudson Street in 1822. It would be here that the poet's memorial service took place on Friday 13 November 1953, immediately before Caitlin Thomas took his body back to Wales. The congregation included Caitlin, e e cummings, William Faulkner, Tennessee Williams and Edith Sitwell. Best of all Dylan liked the White Horse Tavern, a drinking hole for longshoremen a few blocks north on Hudson Street that was built in the 1880s and reminded him of a Welsh dockside pub. Today it is still decorated as the poet last saw it.

Dylan Thomas was one of those writers who played up to the part of the demonic, drink-fuelled roaring boyo. Sadly, he died that way too. No Dylan pilgrimage can entirely avoid a strain of melancholy.

PIERREPONT STREET, NEW YORK – ARTHUR MILLER (1915–2005)

Brooklyn Heights sits directly across the East River from Manhattan and in 1965 became New York's first protected Historic District. Long before then, it had already made its own kind of history as the city's premier bohemian neighbourhood. Henry Miller, author of *Tropic of Cancer* and *Tropic of Capricorn*, lived in Brooklyn Heights in the 1920s. He moved into 91 Remsen Street in 1924, only to be evicted the following year for non-payment of rent. Novelist Thomas Wolfe lived on Montague Terrace in the 1930s, as did W.H. Auden in 1940. Truman Capote rented the basement apartment at 70 Willow Street for ten years in the late 50s and early 60s. Here he finished *Breakfast at Tiffany's* and wrote *In Cold Blood*, as well as penning the essay 'Brooklyn Heights: A Personal Memoir', which includes a line still much enjoyed by locals: 'I live in Brooklyn. By choice.'

But for me the most interesting and productive address in this tree-lined neighbourhood is 102 Pierrepont Street, a house divided into apartments where in 1943 and 1944 young Norman Mailer lived with his parents when home from serving in the Second World War. Meanwhile, in the wood-panelled duplex below lived a writer, eight years his senior, who was exempted from war service by an old sporting injury and struggling with his career. Arthur Miller had moved in recently with his first wife Mary and young daughter, and was seriously considering abandoning drama. In November 1944 his play *The Man Who Had All the Luck* ran for just four performances at the Forest Theatre on Broadway. Over the next three years in Pierrepont Street, Miller worked to discover his dramatic voice, which he did finally in 1947 with *All My Sons*. This play about a factory owner accused of making faulty parts for military planes ran for almost a year at the very same Broadway theatre (albeit renamed the Coronet) and won the New York Drama Critics' Circle Award.

Norman Mailer, returned from serving in the Philippines and working on his war novel, *The Naked and the Dead*, went to see it and later recalled meeting Miller by the ground-floor mailboxes. 'I could write a play like that,' Mailer told Miller. Arthur Miller just laughed. Mailer later recorded: 'I can remember thinking. This guy's never going anywhere. I'm sure he thought the same of me.'

By 1949 Miller had moved to Grace Court, a cul de sac overlooking the East River where he finished *Death of a Salesman*, the big theatrical success of that year, winning both the Pulitzer Prize for Drama and the Tony Award for Best Play. Miller was able to purchase the townhouse at Grace Court and even sublet the bottom two floors to the president of the Brooklyn Savings Bank, thereby further stabilising his income (although the playwright ultimately grew tired of being a landlord).

In 1951, while trying to sell a screenplay to Hollywood, Arthur Miller had a brief extra-marital affair with Marilyn Monroe and afterwards kept in touch with her. In 1956, after writing *The Crucible*, he left his wife Mary for Marilyn, selling Grace Court to W.E.B. DuBois, the African-American activist.

By the early 1960s Arthur Miller's rollercoaster years married to Marilyn were over and he holed up across the

Photo: Autopilot

river in New York's Fashion District at the bohemian (to put it mildly) Hotel Chelsea, where he lamented there wasn't even a vacuum cleaner.

One hot sunny day in August, when the trees offered islands of welcome shade on Pierrepont Street, I went to look at number 102. I also passed by Grace Court, but it was Pierrepont Street that drew me because it was here that his career took off. I suppose it was the appeal of seeing where Arthur Miller licked his wounds after the failure of *The Man Who Had All the Luck* and turned his career around, writing *All My Sons* while Norman Mailer slept upstairs in his parents' spare bedroom.

What surprised me was that 102 is the only house in this long row of Brooklyn Brownstones with a white facade. It seems to take its colour scheme from the marble of the courthouse opposite. The position of the five floors, windows and balconies matches exactly those of the two adjacent houses and all three share a roof as part of one development, but balconies and windows are not original. In fact No. 102 has been modernised at some stage in the twentieth century.

I liked the symbolism in this: Arthur Miller, the man who modernised the American play, working in a house that itself was breaking with local traditions. I also came away thinking there was something symbolic in how Arthur Miller kept on moving house. He had five homes in Brooklyn between 1940 and 1955, a restless fifteen years when he was trying to find himself as a writer. And there's something horribly symbolic too in the fact that he then crossed the river to Manhattan where he ended up living in Marilyn Monroe's Waldorf Tower apartment before spiralling downwards to recuperate in Hotel Chelsea in the 1960s.

Arthur Miller's success continued, but here in Brooklyn Heights was where the great work was done.

LOWELL, MASSACHUSETTS – JACK KEROUAC (1922–69)

'Everyone goes home in October,' wrote Jack Kerouac and so one chilly autumn in New York I decided to do just that – not to my home, but his. It was a four-hour drive north along Interstate 95 to Lowell, reversing the route that Jack would have taken when he headed on the road to Columbia University in 1940.

Jean-Louis Kérouac (known as Ti'Jean in his French-speaking family) was born and raised in Pawtucketville on the north side of the Merrimack River in the old cotton town of Lowell. Eventually he returned to live out his last years here, drinking noisily and growing maudlin. He died in Florida but was brought back and buried in what he always referred to as 'My Lowell'.

Lowell is very quiet these days, and picturesque in a post-industrial way. I got there mid-morning as the sun was illuminating a huge rooftop sign over the *Lowell Sun* newspaper building. Jack Kerouac, the man who gave voice to America's Beat Generation, worked here 75 years ago. Today it stands huge and empty.

Bright sunlight was also picking out the large clock hanging outside Lowell High School. For four years Jack was a student in this extremely long, yellow brick Art Deco building. He claimed he used to smoke beneath its 'boxlike' clock.

Once upon a time Lowell had been hugely important to the Massachusetts economy, with a population big enough to bring Dickens here on a reading tour. Then the Depression ripped the industrial heart out of the town. By the 1940s when Jack first headed out 'on the road', the city was so poor

Photo: Rus bowden

it couldn't afford to demolish its empty old buildings. But this has made Lowell special today. It doesn't look like all the other cookie-cutter American cities with identikit shopping malls. The nearest Starbucks and Dunkin' Donuts are a mile out of town.

Although Jack Kerouac criss-crossed America in the 1950s, questing for something always beyond the horizon – even ending up in Morocco with Allen Ginsberg and William Burroughs at one point – he claimed Lowell remained the most interesting place he knew. Many of his early novels were set here.

I drove on, over the red metal bridge linking the centre of Lowell with Pawtucketville, to look at the simple wooden house where Jack was born and where he made his first stabs at thinly-veiled fiction. No. 9 Lupine Road is a modest two-family house with verandas top and bottom and two front doors side by side, one for the family downstairs and one for the family up top. Jack's parents started off down below but he was born after they moved above. Upstairs was more desirable as heat rises, and in Massachusetts winters you need all the heat you can find.

Crossing back over the Merrimack Canal I came to the New City Hall and the Pollard Memorial Library where Jack – playing hooky from school – determined to read every book in stock. Jack Kerouac was a consummate absentee. He skipped school for 40 days in his final year but still gained a place at Columbia University.

I pushed open the two sets of double doors to enter a smart wood-panelled reading room with chandeliers. 'I saw that my life was a vast glowing empty page,' Kerouac recorded. 'And I could do anything I wanted.'

Looking in the library's local history section I read that Lowell went through some bad times in the 1940s and 50s.

It had a reputation for drugs and violence and soldiers from Fort Devens came here looking – successfully – for prostitutes. But this library would inspire a young man with literary aspirations.

At the Patrick J. Morgan Cultural Center on French Street I saw Jack's typewriter on which in 1951 he pounded out his masterwork, *On the Road*. It's a classic black skeletal Underwood with the keys like little white petri dishes and the H and J badly discoloured. *On the Road* was finally published in 1957 and made Jack a literary star. Sadly success did not make him happy.

Jack bequeathed a lot to Lowell, including a whole archive of his own papers that are still being sifted. Despite his celebrity and restlessness he was repeatedly drawn back to this empty city with its huge, idle red-brick cotton mills. The saddest thing I read here was one of his friends recording that the last time Jack visited Lowell, 'he wanted to be a big kid again and play with the boys for a few days. But the others had grown up, had responsibilities, and Kerouac went away disappointed.'

Jack, like many twentieth-century writers, drank heavily. When he moved back to Lowell he drank at the Sack Club on Market Street. He also drank at Nicky's strip joint on Gorham Street and it was the owner's sister, Stella Sampas, whom he took as his third wife in 1966, confirming his return home. Nicky's is now Ricardo's Café Trattoria and, when I pulled over in my hire car, it looked much more respectable these days although it was shuttered and not yet open for lunch.

From here I thought about heading to the Kerouac grave, but first I walked to 'Funeral Row', Jack's nickname for Pawtucket Street on which still stand Lowell's four funeral homes. Three of them were Irish and one French, Archambault and Sons, which would be the site of Kerouac's wake in 1969.

By early afternoon I made it to Edson Cemetery and the simple stone which records Jack's dates and adds the epitaph 'He Honored Life'. Yes he did, in his own troubled way.

* * *

TOULOUSE STREET, NEW ORLEANS – TENNESSEE WILLIAMS (1911–83)

Certain cities seem to attract writers. In the early twentieth century a lot of authors were drawn to Paris where they could drink cheaply and sexuality was only loosely policed. Berlin under the Weimar Republic offered similar inducements, and so for decades has New Orleans, where – uniquely in the United States – you can stand on a street corner with an alcoholic beverage in your hand and not get arrested. This freedom still pertains today (which can make it very difficult walking through the French Quarter because the streets are clogged with Americans taking full advantage of this uncommon liberty).

Literary greats to enjoy New Orleans' hospitality include William Faulkner, Truman Capote, Kate Chopin, Sherwood Anderson and John Steinbeck. Ernest Hemingway, Lafcadio Hearn, Eudora Welty and Anne Rice also drew inspiration from New Orleans, as did Thomas Lanier ('Tennessee') Williams III.

It was inevitable that I'd be drawn to a city with such a pedigree for writing and alcohol. On my first night in New Orleans I was seriously jetlagged but my American in-laws had insisted I try the famous Gumbo Shop. The gumbo was satisfyingly thick and sustaining after my international flight, a domestic hop from Atlanta, and then a hire-car journey into N'Awlins.

What I didn't realise as I consumed this rich dark stew was that I was already in Literary New Orleans. Next door to the Gumbo Shop at 632 Rue St Peter was a shop called Fleurty Girl. And above that was where Williams worked on *A Streetcar Named Desire*. In my jetlagged state, I had missed the dark metal plaque.

Like many of these French Quarter houses, 632 Rue St Peter is a brick structure with white door frames and the most enormous roofed balcony above. The plaque explained that this was the Avart-Perretti house built in 1842, and the long-term home of the Italian painter-cum-anarchist Achille Peretti. He died here in 1923.

In 1946 Tennessee Williams moved in to rewrite his script of *Streetcar*. He had already emerged from obscurity in 1944 with *The Glass Menagerie* but when *Streetcar* opened in December 1947 it was a huge Broadway success, immediately confirming Williams as one of the greatest American dramatists of his generation. What interested me, however, were the years before his first two successes.

Williams had arrived in New Orleans at the end of 1938, around the same time as he adopted 'Tennessee' as his professional name. Though born in Columbus, Mississippi, the playwright honoured his father's Tennessee pioneer forebears in that choice. Unfortunately Cornelius Coffin Williams of Mississippi did not think well of his son's theatrical aspirations, nor of his sexual orientation, and teased him mercilessly for his effeminate qualities, calling him 'Miss Nancy'.

A week after his arrival the 27-year-old found himself an attic apartment over a shabby restaurant at 722 Toulouse Street. Here in one of the oldest sections of the Vieux Carré he began work on an autobiographical play about a young man struggling with his sexuality and his desire to

Photo: © Kelly Thompson

be a writer. He called the play *Vieux Carré* but laid it aside to work on *Battle of Angels,* his first professionally-produced play, which failed spectacularly when staged in 1940 but was reworked successfully in 1957 as *Orpheus Descending.*

This was the building I wanted to see. Toulouse Street is just three blocks from where I was staying at the Monteleone, so the next day I walked round to look at the garret where an uncertain young playwright proved that he could make money out of writing, pulling together the painful autobiographical strands that would eventually form *The Glass Menagerie.*

Today 722 Toulouse Street is part of the Historic New Orleans Collection complex and contains the archives of the association, which functions as a museum, research centre and publisher, dedicated to preserving the city's heritage. Toulouse Street itself is lined with some of New Orleans' original single-storey eighteenth-century cottages, but No. 722 is two storeys, with the garret making it three.

Entrance to the Historic New Orleans Collection is actually on Royal Street, which is where I picked up a brochure that told me – among many other things – that Tennessee's first home in New Orleans had been built in 1788 by a Mr Louis Adam but by the 1930s it was in a sorry state and functioning as a boarding house.

At the back of 722 there is a staircase – partly external – that leads up to 'Tennessee's room'. It isn't open to the public but I managed to see around. There's a lot of storage up there but the layout recalled the description Tennessee wrote down when he resumed work on *Vieux Carré* in 1977: 'A curved staircase ascends from the rear of a dark narrow passageway from the street entrance.' Up in the attic there were indeed 'a pair of alcoves facing on to Toulouse Street'; Tennessee claimed these were partitioned off by plywood in his day to make two rooms. In *Vieux Carré* the young writer lives in one of these attic rooms, and an old painter, dying of tuberculosis, in the other. At the back of the attic, separated off by a narrow hallway, was a studio with a skylight where lived two more people. In *Vieux Carré* they are Jane, a New Rochelle society girl dying of leukaemia, and her sexually ambiguous lover, Tye. In its barrenness, Tennessee wrote, 'there is a poetic evocation of all the cheap rooming houses of the world'.

Vieux Carré was not a financial success but for Tennessee enthusiasts it's a tellingly autobiographical play about those early days in New Orleans. In that store-room I caught just a hint of the time when this *was* Tennessee's room. I felt I could have stayed here, moved a few boxes and done some writing myself. New Orleans appeals to the writer in us all.

HOTEL MONTELEONE, NEW ORLEANS – TRUMAN CAPOTE (1924–84)

Truman Capote often claimed he was born at New Orleans' Hotel Monteleone. Sometimes he even claimed that he was born at its rotating Carousel Bar. This was definitely untrue, as it wasn't constructed until 1949. What we do know is that Truman's seventeen-year-old mother was staying at the Monteleone at the time of his birth, but the hotel got her to the Touro Infirmary in time for the little literary genius to be delivered. However, there remains a poetic truth in the statement. The Carousel Bar at the Monteleone could be seen as Truman's spiritual home and the hotel as his godfather. Truman needed godfathers. A metaphorical

Photo: © Kate Tadman-Mourby

search for absent fathers can be traced through much of his literature.

Glitzy, bustling, and remarkably tall for New Orleans, the Monteleone is like a piece of New York hotel real restate transplanted to this European city on the banks of the Mississippi. It was developed from 1886 onwards by Antonio Monteleone, an Italian immigrant shoemaker whose family still owns the 600-bedroom block. Massively enlarged in the 1950s and 60s, the Monteleone remains the only high-rise in the old French Quarter. With its roots firmly in the Beaux Arts movement, it continues to be the place to stay in New Orleans. Tennessee Williams mentions it in *The Rose Tattoo* and *Orpheus Descending*, Eudora Welty cites it in *A Curtain of Green*, Hemingway refers to it in his short story *Night Before Battle*, and Rebecca Wells features it in *The Divine Secrets of the Ya-Ya Sisterhood*.

According to Truman, during a very lonely childhood his mother would sometimes lock him in her suite at the Monteleone while she went out partying for the evening. Later, after his parents' divorce, when he was sent to live with his cousins in Alabama, Truman would still come back to the French Quarter for holidays. In the 1940s, as a beautiful blond young man with literary ambitions, Truman worked on his first novel, *Other Voices, Other Rooms* at 711a Royal Street, New Orleans. Thanks to word of mouth and Truman's own conspicuous showmanship, the book was a runaway literary success even before it was printed in 1948. Tellingly, the story focused on a lonely and slightly effeminate thirteen-year-old boy sent away from New Orleans to live with the father who had abandoned him at the time of his birth.

Today you can find where Truman wrote *Other Voices, Other Rooms* between the hat shop at 709 Royal Street and the shop for locally printed T-shirts at No. 713. There is a passageway that runs down past an old dark staircase leading up to apartments, and into a brick courtyard. Antiques are sold in the passageway and impeded my way, but I found the courtyard itself, screened off by two large shutters with the words 'PRIVATE COURTYARD – PLEASE NO PHOTOS' neatly chalked on one of them. Clearly, a lot of pilgrims come here. Nevertheless I peeped over the shutters and through the gap between them to see a small white-balconied house surrounded by plant pots where Truman wrote his first bestseller. From old photos I've seen, it was definitely scruffier – and cheaper – in his day. Today it's about as bijou as even Truman would have wanted.

Truman Capote continued to visit New Orleans, sometimes to retreat from the fame he so strenuously courted – especially after the film of *Breakfast at Tiffany's* made him a twinkling star in the 1960s. He also lived for a while in Rome in Via Margutta very close to where Keats died, but he retained a fondness for the French Quarter. In a 1981 interview in *People* magazine, long after the non-fiction novel *In Cold Blood* had made Truman a major force in modern literature, he said: 'I get seized by a mood and I go. I stay a few weeks and I read and write and walk around. It's like a hometown to me.' He then went on to praise St Louis cathedral, the Caribbean Room at the Pontchartrain Hotel, and the Bourbon Street burlesque club Gunga Den as some of his favourite sights.

Like Truman I have enjoyed sitting on one of the bar stools at the glitzy Carousel Bar, which moves on 2,000 rollers and looks remarkably like a fairground carousel. It makes one very slow rotation every fifteen minutes. It's easy to imagine him perched on one of these stools, his legs dangling and his strange, high-pitched voice dominating the bar.

Today Truman would probably be thrilled to know that there is a Capote Suite at the Monteleone. It's one of five literary suites that the hotel created in honour of its most famous literary guests – Faulkner, Tennessee Williams, Hemingway, Welty and Truman. When I got myself invited to take a look I thought it rather restrained and its curtains over-ruched. My wife's New England grandmother would like it, but the décor is probably a wise choice: not all guests at the Monteleone would share Truman Capote's unique talent and florid taste.

ST PETERSBURG

REKI MOYKI – ALEXANDER PUSHKIN (1799–1837)

Alexander Pushkin's last home was a first-floor apartment on Reki Moyki, in the house of Prince Pyotr Volkonsky overlooking the Moika River. It's a big cream-painted building with white piping like so many in St Petersburg. It wasn't uncommon for a noble family to rent out parts of their property portfolio. Volkonsky, a hero of Napoleon's defeat in 1812, was now a Minister of the Imperial Court and in 1834 had been given the title Serene Highness by Tsar Nicholas I. Two years later the Pushkins became his tenants. Their occupancy would run only four months because on 10 February 1837 (29 January Old Calendar) Alexander Pushkin died in this apartment from gunshot wounds.

The darling of the St Petersburg literary scene was killed duelling over a woman, just like Lensky in Pushkin's great narrative poem, *Eugene Onegin*. As with Onegin and Lensky, the argument was between men who should have been friends; Pushkin challenged his wife's brother-in-law, Georges d'Anthès, after rumours spread that d'Anthès was her lover. The Frenchman only made matters worse when he published a lampoon that referred to Pushkin as 'Deputy Grand Master and Historiographer of the Order of Cuckolds'.

Pushkin was devoted to his beautiful wife Natalya; it was to make her happy that he had allowed them to stumble into

Photo: Adrian Mourby

debts in St Petersburg. This was a difficult time in the poet's life. He was grieving for the loss of his mother, coping with inheritance issues and working hard to keep a magazine that he had founded, *Sovremennik* (The Contemporary), going.

Not yet 40, Pushkin was being talked of as the father of modern Russian literature but he was not financially astute. Instead of publishing his new historical novel *The Captain's Daughter* (1836) as a book and making money, he serialised it in *Sovremennik* and made nothing. At his death Pushkin left two unfinished short stories, *The Story of the Village of Goryukhino* and *Egyptian Nights*, as well as two more novels, *Roslavlev* and *Dubrovsky* – all worked on here but none completed.

I picture him exhausted as he wrote into the night at his slender wooden desk overlooking the Moika River, struggling to stay solvent. It was reckless of him to challenge d'Anthès. Unfortunately, although duelling was strictly illegal in Tsarist Russia, it was still expected when men of honour clashed. Pushkin had fought duels successfully before. But his family – and Russian literature – really needed him to stay alive.

It was a cruelly cold February when I visited St Petersburg. The sun was bright but ice formed in my beard as I walked past the Lutheran church of SS Peter and Paul and the Hermitage Museum. When I turned onto the embankment itself, a vicious wind stung my cheeks. Was it this cold the afternoon that Pushkin and d'Anthès duelled among the dachas outside St Petersburg?

Snow was piled up high in the courtyard of the old Volkonsky mansion, part of which has been the Pushkin Museum since 1925. On the ground floor I found a cloakroom and a useful introduction to Pushkin's life and the story of his death. Talking to the curator I also learned that I had only just missed its annual commemoration of his demise which, since 1925, is marked in this very courtyard.

Here representatives of the city's administration, members of the scientific and creative communities of St Petersburg, and Pushkin's descendants (there are many) stand in silence at 2.45pm, the moment when the poet's heart ceased beating.

The museum has recreated Pushkin's apartment as it looked in 1836–7 just before the duel. To do this they used contemporary sketches made by the poet Vasily Zhukovsky and drew on written recollections of Pushkin's friends. That the museum survived the appalling Siege of Leningrad (as St Petersburg was then called) in 1941–4 says a lot for the priority accorded to literature by the Russian people. It also says a lot for the Russian ability to reconstruct. Photos of the city, which had been bombed and starved almost to death by the Wehrmacht and Luftwaffe for 872 days, show how completely the St Petersburg of Tolstoy, Pushkin and Dostoyevsky had to be rebuilt after the Second World War.

The main room of the apartment is Pushkin's working study, lined with his possessions or facsimiles. The custodian told me rather poetically that here there were many things 'that remember the touch of his hands'. I looked at his red leather chair and sofa, and his delicate writing desk with the paper knife he chewed, and an inkstand in black and gold. It depicted a negro figure that the custodian said was a memento of Pushkin's Central African ancestor, Gannibal, who in the eighteenth century rose to be superintendent of Tallinn under Empress Elizabeth of Russia. I also saw a small portrait of Natalia Pushkina, so beautiful that it was said she was briefly the mistress of the Tsar after her husband's untimely death.

So often these writers' rooms are tinged with sadness, especially when the author died too soon. What might John Keats have gone on to write in Piazza di Spagna if his tuberculosis had been curable in 1821? What if Virginia

Woolf's intense depression had not driven her to suicide while she was staying at Monk's House? What if Dylan Thomas hadn't drunk himself to death at Hotel Chelsea? Similarly with Pushkin. He left this room on 27 January for a duel that would have taken place with the same insistence on form that Tolstoy would soon record in *War and Peace* and Pushkin himself had already described in *Eugene Onegin*. Sadly, Alexander Pushkin did not die instantly like poor Lensky, but lingered for two days with a bullet wound in his abdomen.

Surprised by the liberal outpouring of grief that greeted news of his death, the Tsarist authorities obliged Pushkin's grieving family to remove his body overnight to his mother's estate in the Pskow region, where he was quietly buried on 6 February.

He was only 37, a father of four young children and with many more years of great writing in him. No wonder St Petersburg's intelligentsia bow their heads in the cold, wintry courtyard every year.

KUZNECHNYY PEREULOK – FYODOR DOSTOYEVSKY (1821–81)

Maybe I shouldn't have seen them on the same day, but after the grace and decorum of Pushkin's apartment, Fyodor Dostoyevsky's was disappointing. Of course it provided an insight into the man, but if Pushkin's was the apartment of an early nineteenth-century dandy, Dostoyevsky's to me was the last home of a big shaggy man who by all accounts cared deeply about keeping his desk tidy but had a lamentable fondness for Russian Victoriana.

Fyodor Dostoyevsky rented apartment 5/2 at Kuznechnyy Pereulok (Kuznechnyy Lane) twice in his troubled life, once for a very short period in 1846, and then from October 1878 until his death in January 1881. It was here that he wrote his last great novel, *The Brothers Karamazov.*

Kuznechnyy Lane is in Tsentralny District, not far from St Petersburg's main railway station. I found this very apt. Between Pushkin's time and Dostoyevsky's the railways arrived in Russia – and entered dramatically into Russian fiction. In *The Demons* Verkhovensky flees on a train, in *The Brothers Karamazov* Kolya boldly lies between railroad tracks as a train passes over him, and in *The Gambler* Alexei sees his grandmother off at a railway station. *The Idiot* opens with Prince Lev Nikolayevich Myshkin returning to Russia on a train. Trains are also to be found in Tolstoy's work, most dramatically in *Anna Karenina.* Pushkin was only 22 years older than Dostoyevsky and 29 years older than Tolstoy, but he inhabited a Russia of elegant horse-drawn carriages, they of smoky railway carriages and noisy engines.

Even today with the wholesale gentrification of St Petersburg, Kuznechnyy Lane is unprepossessing. Inside, the Dostoyevskys' apartment has been recreated for the most part from the memoirs of his second wife Anna, and of his contemporaries. It was opened on 12 November 1971 when the city was still called Leningrad. The apartment takes up the corner wing of a dull, four-storey city block typical of the kind you find across Europe, built quickly and built tall as cities grew rapidly in the latter half of the nineteenth century.

The author's study is decorated with a greenish wallpaper with a repeated floral scroll patterning that would drive you crazy if you stared at it for too long. Historians found this under eighteen other layers of more recent wallpaper and had it recreated for the museum as the most period-

Photo: Davide Mauro

appropriate. Near his big, heavy wooden desk with its little fat legs stands a big black clock – stopped at the hour that he died. Roll-up cigarettes of the kind Dostoyevsky smoked lie on another table which is covered with a green cloth. The floor is scuffed parquet.

I'd read that Dostoyevsky liked the corners of buildings. The wider views meant he could see the nearby domes of Our Lady of Vladimir church. Although Dostoyevsky had to move frequently because of his debts, I gather he always tried to find an apartment with a view of a church or cathedral.

The dining room has a big white ceramic-tiled heater in the corner and its table was draped in a white cloth with ragged tassels. The overly-ornate crockery on display reminded me of the kind my great aunts inherited from their mothers. There was a small rocking horse by the hearth. Between 1868 and 1875 Dostoyevsky's wife bore four children, two of whom died in infancy. I also saw Dostoyevsky's hat on show inside a glass case and two of his umbrellas in a stand in the hall.

With the help of the museum downstairs I was able to piece together Dostoyevsky's life and what he wrote in the apartment above. His first novel *Poor Folk*, described at the time as Russia's first 'social novel', was published in January 1846 and was a much-needed commercial success for the 24-year-old aspiring writer. He then resigned his military career and wrote a second novel, *The Double*, in which the main character descends into insanity. It was not well reviewed. Around this time Dostoyevsky discovered French ideas of socialism and in this apartment he began a new novel, *Netochka Nezvanova* ('Nameless Nobody'), about a young St Petersburg woman living in extreme poverty, but he never completed it.

On 23 April 1849 Dostoyevsky was one of a number of idealistic writers arrested on the orders of Tsar Nicolas I.

By the time he returned to live in Kuznechnyy Pereulok in 1878 he had experienced a life as desperate as any of his characters. Aged 56 he could look back on narrowly escaping execution by firing squad for his political views, spending five years in bleak Siberian exile that permanently damaged his health, marrying, and losing both his wife and his first child, becoming addicted to gambling, losing nearly all his money as a result, and embarking on a number of extramarital affairs. Yet he had also become a literary success. With *The House of the Dead* (1862), *Notes from the Underground* (1864), *Crime and Punishment* (1866), *The Gambler* (1867), *The Idiot* (1868) and *The Adolescent* (1875) behind him, Fyodor Dostoyevsky was working on his final book. He spent nearly two years writing the twelve-volume philosophical novel, *The Brothers Karamazov*, which was first published as a serial from January 1879 to November 1880. This makes the study at Kuznechnyy Lane very much Dostoyevsky's *Karamazov* room. It is a great work of literature, but how could he manage to concentrate in such an ugly apartment?

These quests for an author's writing room can bring one up against one's own prejudices. I felt I would have written wittily and elegantly in Pushkin's apartment. Sitting in Dostoyevsky's I think I would have decamped to the nearest café. Clearly he and I could never have decorated a house together.

Fyodor Dostoyevsky died at Kuznechnyy Lane less than four months after the publication of *The Brothers Karamazov*, suffering the first of his three heart attacks when a neighbour's apartment was raided by the Tsarist police. I came away disliking the bourgeois dullness of that ugly apartment, yet after such a dramatic and difficult life, it was probably what Dostoyevsky craved.

HOTEL ASTORIA – MIKHAIL BULGAKOV (1891–1940)

According to Mikhail Bulgakov, Room 412 on the fourth floor of the Hotel Astoria is 'a room, where, as is well known, there is blue-gray furniture and a fine bathroom'. That line comes from his novel *The Master and Margarita*, which Bulgakov began in 1928 and completed shortly before his death of a kidney disorder in 1940. The story concerns a visit by the Devil to the atheist Soviet Union and is a satire on the new Russian state. It was a *samizdat* (clandestine) publication, not issued in book form until 1967.

In the 1920s the playwright and novelist Mikhail Afanasyevich Bulgakov suffered greatly from the government's persecution of creative artists. At one point he was frightened enough to burn the first manuscript of *The Master and Margarita*. Bulgakov was fortunate, however, that the unpredictable General Secretary Stalin liked his work despite its un-Soviet attitudes. Stalin protected the author and after he was sacked personally reinstated him in his job at the Moscow Art Theatre.

In 1932, after divorcing his second wife, Bulgakov married Yelena Nyurenberg, who had in turn divorced her army officer husband so that they could be together. The couple honeymooned at the Astoria Hotel in Leningrad that October. At the time of his remarriage Bulgakov had been invited to Leningrad (these days known once again as St Petersburg) on theatre business and so it was a local theatre company who actually footed the bill for their honeymoon. Yelena is generally believed to be the model for Margarita in Bulgakov's most famous novel. She claimed he recommended the story here, dictating fresh chapters to her, and told her:

'The whole world was against me and I was alone. Now we are together, and nothing frightens me.'

The Astoria gets only a brief walk-on role near the end of Bulgakov's novel after Grigory Danilovich Rimsky, treasurer of the Variety Theatre in Moscow, is attacked on the night of the great satanic performance staged by Professor Woland (who is really the Devil in disguise). Rimsky's attacker is Varenukha (house manager of the theatre) who has been temporarily turned into a vampire by Woland. Terrified, Rimsky flees to the railway station and takes a train to Leningrad. He is found later in Room 412 of the Astoria, hiding in a wardrobe and barely sane. He is arrested and brought back to Moscow.

Most people assume that the Bulgakovs themselves stayed in Room 412 and were able to enjoy that in-joke. Sadly if you look for Room 412 today you will not find it, as it was merged into Room 411 some years ago to create a Presidential Suite. However it's clear that Room 412 was at the point where the two wings of the hotel sharply intersect, giving a very good view out across St Isaac's Square from above the front door.

The Astoria remains one of my favourite St Petersburg hotels. It was commissioned in 1910 by the British Palace Hotel Company to accommodate international guests during the tercentenary celebrations of the Romanoff dynasty in 1913. Little did anyone think then that Russia's first family had only four of its 304 years left in power. The architect was Fyodor Lidval, born in St Petersburg to Swedish parents. The style of the building is a kind of stripped-down Art Nouveau that flirts with Art Deco but retreats into neoclassicism, especially in its austere facade. Adolf Hitler, a keen amateur architect, loved this building. During the Siege of Leningrad he insisted it not be bombed even though the nearby St Isaac's cathedral was significantly damaged. The Führer intended to hold his victory banquet

Photo: Andrew Shiva

in the Astoria once Leningrad had fallen, and had even had invitations printed.

For decades after the Second World War the Astoria was run by the state-owned Intourist travel group. It underwent the usual Soviet neglect, which in a way was fortunate. (The auditorium of the St Petersburg Conservatory where Tchaikovsky's opera *Eugene Onegin* was premiered was refurbished under Communism and a priceless Italianate jewel of a theatre was eviscerated by concrete and bad taste.)

In 1987 the hotel was closed for mercifully sympathetic renovations, and it was purchased in 1997 by Rocco Forte Hotels who spent $20 million on further upgrades. Today the Astoria has a 1930s feel to its public spaces, with marble floors and bound fasces – a common 1930s symbol – carved around the bedroom doors. The lift portals on the ground floor to the left of reception display brass door plaques naming the many celebrity guests who have stayed at the Astoria. These included socialists like Lenin and H.G. Wells, actors like Jack Nicholson and Gina Lollobrigida, many world leaders, and musicians like Pavarotti, Madonna and Elton John. Rumour has it that Rasputin stayed here during the last years of the Romanoff empire, with various married women to whom he ministered.

You really cannot get a more celebrated hotel in Russia – and the Astoria is comfortable too. There's not much to give you an insight into Bulgakov and his satiric masterwork, but it's nice to think of him taking up the story again here with Yelena.

EAST ASIA

SHIOMI NAWATE STREET, MATSUE, JAPAN – LAFCADIO HEARN (1850–1904)

My wife is an enthusiast for all things Japanese so we were in Matsue for her. It's a sweet, undersized city on the north coast of southern Honshu with a small castle and boat tours of the inner and outer moats. There is also a samurai residence to visit and the former home of an author who deserves to be better known in the West. Patrick Lafcadio Hearn was born in Greece to an Irish surgeon in the British army and an illiterate Greek mother. Via a series of misfortunes he was abandoned by both parents and most of his relatives. He ended up being raised in Ireland by a very straitlaced aunt and then, as a young man, living rough in London.

At the age of nineteen Lafcadio was sent to America by a relative who thought his in-laws over there might help out. They didn't, but the young man did well as a journalist in Cincinnati where he was known for sensationalist articles and florid descriptions. In due course he moved to an editorial post in New Orleans, where his bright, enquiring mind helped him to write successfully about Creole culture and even produce a local cookbook. The city still preserves his house on Cleveland Avenue.

To find Lafcadio's home in Matsue we followed signs showing a baggy little man carrying tattered suitcases walking ahead of us. This was one of his own self-deprecating

Photo: © Kate Tadman-Mourby

cartoons. On the way my wife filled me in enthusiastically on Lafcadio's life. As a schoolboy he lost an eye in a sporting accident. Later he was sacked by one set of employers for marrying an African-American woman, and another time was banished on a lengthy assignment to the West Indies.

By the time he reached Japan in 1890, Lafcadio Hearn had packed a lot of restless living into his first 40 years. Here he finally, for the first time in his life, found a home. Hearn embraced Japan, married the daughter of a local samurai, taught successfully at the local school, and set about translating Japanese stories into English. He and his wife worked on this project together, she reading tales out to him in pidgin English and he working them into something readable. In the last ten years of his life he produced fifteen books about Japan. Some were translations of ghost stories and legends, others were accounts of his travels and observations about his adopted country for an excited Occidental public. Taking Japanese citizenship (he is known as Koizumi Yakumo in Japan, and is regarded with much affection), Lafcadio Hearn probably did more than any other western writer to make Japan accessible and not just exotic to curious Westerners.

The house where he lived in Matsue has been preserved as a designated Historic Site since 1940. It stands on Shiomi Nawate Street near a sharp bend in the Inner Moat and is traditionally constructed of dark wood with tatami mats and shoji screens. In its grounds stands the Lafcadio Hearn Memorial Museum, which was established in 1933 to explain his work. More than 150,000 people a year visit this shrine to the undersized, half-blind man who found a home in Japan.

We paid our 300 yen to look around, entering through a courtyard of white pebbles. The house was small and bare except for a reproduction of his simple Western-style writing table and a chair, both with the legs linked by wooden runners so they could be slid, like a sledge, across the tatami without scratching it. There was a big shell on the desk and his magnifying glass, which was huge. His one remaining eye was in poor condition.

Old photos showed the room much more cluttered with Victorian bric-a-brac and bookcases everywhere when Lafcadio lived here, but I think the sense of serenity was probably accurate. He stopped travelling when he reached Japan. I could understand why. Out in his small garden – which, unlike the house, has not been refurbished – a very old, rather weary tree was supported by a stone and the pond was full of bright green lilies. I felt I could sit here a while, and in fact we both did.

Every year on 26 September, the anniversary of his death, an English speech recitation contest and a haiku contest are held in Matsue to honour Lafcadio. He is also commemorated in a statue that I spotted across the road as we left. All photos I have seen of the author show him in profile, because he was embarrassed by his missing eye, but this bust has him looking you in the face, both eyes open and clear. It seemed a nice, very Japanese way to honour Koizumi Yakumo.

THE CATHAY HOTEL, SHANGHAI – GEORGE BERNARD SHAW (1856–1950)

By the time George Bernard Shaw arrived in Shanghai he was – thanks to relentless self-promotion – one of the most famous literary men in the world. The tall bearded Irishman's trajectory was cleared for him by the disgrace of his contemporary Oscar

Wilde. Shaw was a Nobel prize-winning playwright, novelist, essayist and polemicist. He was a Fabian, a free-thinker and a stout defender of the rights of the working classes. He was also co-founder of the London School of Economics, had helped to establish the *New Statesman* magazine and was a great enjoyer of life. 'I'm only a beer teetotaller,' Shaw once remarked. 'Not a champagne teetotaller.'

Approaching his eightieth birthday, GBS set off in December 1932 on a cruise to the Far East on board the *Empress of Britain.* He had speaking engagements booked in Manila, Singapore and Hong Kong, as well as a lunch in Shanghai with Madame Sun, widow of Sun Yat Sen, the founding father of the Republic of China. Later – after a rather hairy plane ride over the Great Wall of China, where (to his horror) he saw Chinese and Japanese troops shooting at each other – he would cross the Pacific to America.

The day before his arrival in Shanghai, its Rotary Club members – not the most liberal of expatriates – declared Shaw a 'blighter' and an 'ignoramus' and resolved not to acknowledge his presence in their lucrative colony. Shaw had other plans anyway. Madame Sun had invited him to her spacious 1920s villa at 29 Rue Molière in the French Concession and here Shaw lunched with some of the leading writers and intellectuals of 1930s China. This was a period of great global turbulence – a time in which foreign powers were pushing rival claims on China – but GBS was adamant that he had not come to impose solutions: 'It is not for me, belonging as I do to a quarter of the globe which is mismanaging its affairs in a ruinous fashion to pretend to advise an ancient people striving to set its house in order.'

At that famous lunch on 17 February 1933 Shaw met with the co-founders of the Chinese League for Civil Rights, as well as the Soviet spy Agnes Smedley, the editor and critic of the nationalist government Lin Yutang, and the American journalist Harold Isaacs. The last two were later painted out of the commemorative photograph taken that day – Lin because he moved to America in 1935, and Isaacs because in 1938 he published a damning history of the Chinese Revolution.

The official record of Shaw's visit ends after his departure from the PEN Club meeting that followed the lunch, but from the record of Mr Yang Meng Liang, who wrote his memoirs in 2005, we know that Shaw then stayed on at the Cathay Hotel (now Shanghai's Peace Hotel). At the time Mr Yang worked as hotel doorman.

'In the period of the Anti-Japanese war I was a very humble attendant at Cathay hotel. I saw many different people there. I still remember what the foreign supervisor said to us, "Keep on your work carefully. You know finding 100 guys is much easier than finding 100 dogs." At that hard time, we had to bear the insults and the hard work. I was still a doorman in 1933 when the Irishman, George Bernard Shaw came to Shanghai and visited our hotel.'

Today the Peace Hotel is very proud to have welcomed celebrities like Charlie Chaplin, Noël Coward and Shaw. It also hosted the young, as yet unknown Christopher Isherwood, who in 1938 wrote enthusiastically about the availability of sex in Shanghai, adding: 'You can dance at the Tower Restaurant on the roof of the Cathay Hotel, and gossip with Freddy Kaufmann, its charming manager, about the European aristocracy or pre-Hitler Berlin.'

However, these days the Peace Hotel cannot tell you where Shaw – or any of these literary greats – actually stayed, or which of them met with Sir Victor Sassoon who had built the hotel in 1926. He had a private dining room on the eleventh floor in which visiting celebrities were entertained below the hotel's famous, green conical tower.

Photo: Adrian Mourby

Much of the hotel's archive was lost in 1949 after Sir Victor had slipped away to a life in the Bahamas as Mao's Communist army swept into Shanghai. The old Cathay Hotel was nationalised and then turned into offices. In 1952 it was reopened as a hotel and in 1956 it was renamed Peace Hotel, a cruel appropriation of a seemingly innocent word, given the belligerent behaviour of the revolutionary Chinese government.

After the opening up of the Chinese state in the 1980s, following Deng Xiaoping's declaration that it was 'glorious to get rich', the Peace Hotel was restored to much of its former Art Deco glory and the Canadian hotel giant Fairmont was brought in to manage it.

One morning in 2009 I arrived there in the company of an international posse of hard-drinking journalists. We had been brought in overnight to see the beauty of the restored Cathay/Peace Hotel but one of our number had discovered a bottle of absinthe on the flight and no one was in a good frame of mind. We probably looked just like the kind of decadent Eurotrash that Isherwood and Mr Yang Meng Liang recalled from 1930s Shanghai.

In the days that followed I learned a lot about the Peace Hotel and how it had been built as Sassoon House, the first skyscraper in the Far East. Its ground floor had been given over to banks and shops with offices above. The fourth through to ninth floors once housed the Cathay Hotel and the top floor, originally Sassoon's own penthouse apartment, was now the hotel's Sassoon Suite. What I did not discover was where GBS sat and slept and recharged his formidable batteries. At the time he was writing his plays *The Simpleton of the Unexpected Isles* and *The Six of Calais*.

Shaw's visit had a surprisingly large impact on China. Today the study of his works continues in Chinese universities in the way that it certainly doesn't in Britain. At Fudan University there is an annual Shaw essay competition.

Although evidence of the man eluded me in Shanghai, I did learn a great deal about Sir Victor's hotel with its marble foyers and Lalique chandeliers, and it was easy to imagine GBS enjoying himself at the old Cathay Hotel. Shaw was, after all, one of those Fabian socialists who believed everyone – rather than no one – should be able to drink champagne.

THE ORIENTAL HOTEL, BANGKOK – W. SOMERSET MAUGHAM (1874–1965)

The Oriental Hotel in Bangkok was originally just a few rooms and a lot of verandas on the banks of the busy Chao Phraya River. It was built by a consortium of Danish sea captains responding to the need for European sailors to have somewhere to stay, now that the Kingdom of Siam was opening up to trade. The establishment of a 'River Wing' in 1877 is generally held to be the date when the hotel became the institution we know today.

Many itinerant writers stayed in the Oriental's River Wing in its early days, including Joseph Conrad, Somerset Maugham and Noël Coward (who, like Hemingway, homed in on all the best hotels). Maugham recalled that on one occasion he was almost ejected from his room at the Oriental because the manager thought he was about to die of malaria. That story went into his semi-fictional Far East travelogue *The Gentleman in the Parlour*, published in 1930.

You have to look for the old River Wing if you visit today. In 1976 the Oriental built a new multi-storey block which was

cleverly angled so that every room looked down the Chao Phraya. They named this block the River Wing, while the old part of the hotel was renamed the Writers' Wing, with a tea room on the ground floor and suites in honour of its most celebrated writers on the first. I always wanted to stay in one of these, but the closest I got on my two journeys through Thailand was being shown round by the management.

The Somerset Maugham Suite wasn't necessarily where Maugham stayed in 1923 – the year of his malaria – but it might have been, and in any case it had a similar layout. There was a very large mirror, a low 1920s dressing table and a double bed with a mosquito net draped on a frame over it.

A photo taken in the 1920s looks similar except there were two single beds, which would have been used by Maugham and Frederick Gerald Haxton, his American secretary and long-term lover. In his travel stories Maugham invariably depicts himself as the lone wanderer, but in fact, just as Hemingway always travelled with a wife (who was usually written out of his rogue-male narratives), so Maugham took most of his journeys with the gregarious, ebullient Haxton, who chatted to all the locals so that the shy, insular Maugham would have something to write about.

When I peeked into the Maugham Suite I could see the room he described in Chapter 31 of *The Gentleman in the Parlour*: 'My room faced the river. It was dark, one of a long line with a veranda on each side of it, the breeze blew through but it was stifling.' Maugham also disliked the dining room at the Oriental, where guests were 'waited on by silent Chinese boys', and the 'insipid Eastern food' sickened him. He found the heat overwhelming and soon fell ill, his temperature reaching 105. Having trained as a doctor, he knew immediately it was malaria.

One day, lying feverish in his room, Maugham overheard Madame Maire, the manageress of the Oriental telling the local doctor:

'I can't have him die here, you know. You must take him to hospital.'

The doctor suggested they gave it a day or two.

'Well don't leave it too long!'

In *The Gentleman in the Parlour*, Maugham recovers after a few days, 'and because I had nothing to do except look at the river and enjoy the weakness that held me blissfully to my chair I invented a fairy story'.

That story is told in Chapter 32 of his travelogue. However, Paul Theroux has proved that the story, 'Princess September', had been written before Maugham and Haxton set off on their journey from Europe. (We expect writers to be good at their craft and we like them to be inspired by their surroundings, but we can't expect them to be honest as well.)

Like Maugham, I have spent many hours looking at the Chao Phraya River while staying at the Oriental Hotel. Actually I have only ever stayed at the *Mandarin* Oriental because in 1985 it merged with the Mandarin in Hong Kong to become one of the flagships of a new hotel company.

My rooms have always been in the modern River Wing where there are suites dedicated to writers who visited later – Wilbur Smith, John Le Carré, and Barbara Cartland.

But I always hoped that one day I'd stay in one of the suites in the Writers' Wing and recapture the view that had inspired Maugham. The Chao Phraya is an ever-changing urban theatre, like the Bosphorus at Istanbul or the Grand Canal in Venice. I particularly loved the hotel's teakwood shuttle boats that ferry guests to dinner on the far shore.

Sadly it never happened. When I returned in 2016, en route to Cambodia, I was sorry to hear the writer suites had been swept away in a refurbishment to create a new Royal Suite on the first floor of the Writers' Wing. Downstairs, however, new lounges have been created to preserve the names of Conrad, Coward and Maugham as well as James Michener and the Thai writer, Khun Ankana. The large ornate mirror that hitherto dominated Maugham's suite is now the focal point in a lounge, full of white wicker armchairs, named after him.

A Writers' Wall has also been created in what is now called The Writers' Lounge, on which is displayed a rotating collection of framed photos donated by the many scribblers to have stayed at the Oriental. I was mollified to see my own picture up there. How long it remained after I checked out I've no idea, but I certainly appreciated the gesture.

HOTEL CONTINENTAL, SAIGON – GRAHAM GREENE (1904–91)

The Hotel Continental in Saigon sits opposite a very Parisian-looking opera house. Both face what used to be called Place Garnier but is now Lam Son Square in the renamed Ho Chi Minh City. When you come to Vietnam you get used to most things not being called what they once were, but I'm glad the famous Hotel Continental is unchanged. That said, I wouldn't have minded if the levels of service or comfort had improved since the 1950s, but you can't have everything.

On checking in one typically humid day in the summer of 2010, I waited and sweltered while a handwritten account was laboriously taken of my credit card number. I was then left to carry my own luggage to the third floor where I found a wide internal veranda running around the landing. A housekeeper clad in a boiler suit got up slowly from his desk, led me to my room and opened the door for me. He then looked expectantly at me until I tipped him. According to my guidebook, tipping was an alien concept to the Vietnamese but this man had mastered the basics admirably.

My room was spacious but devoid of decoration. It held a desk, two large single beds and two huge carved rocking chairs and that, apart from an arthritic fan in the ceiling, was that. I opened the French windows on to my tiny balcony and they squeaked and juddered. The roar of motor scooters down below filled the room. When I looked out along the hotel's facade I found my window was next to the faded H of the sign 'Grand Hotel Continental'. The Continental may no longer claim to be grand but if you've read any Graham Greene it is wonderfully evocative of his shabby, compromised world.

The hotel opened in 1886. André Malraux stayed here in the 1920s when he was starting his anti-colonial newspaper *Indochine*. The legendary US reporter and anchorman Walter Cronkite stayed here too while reporting on what is known in Vietnam as 'The American War.' But my reason for coming to the Continental was to write an article for CNN about Graham Greene, who in 1952 holed up here to start a novel about the genesis of that disastrous conflict.

The Quiet American took him over two years to complete and was published in 1955. Greene already knew Vietnam well, having worked as a war correspondent in Indo-China for both *The Times* and *Le Figaro*. The Grand Hotel Continental features heavily in his book and also in its subsequent film adaptations. In Greene's day the hotel was owned by Mathieu Francini, a Corsican gangster. Now it belongs to the state, like much else in Vietnam. In the 1950s it was distinctly

Photo: Franklin Heijnen

louche. It still is. My stay there was by turns atmospheric, grim, fascinating and hilarious.

After a much-needed shower I lay down to rest on one of the hard wooden beds. On the bedside table I found a list of 25 charges intended to deter visitors from pilfering. These ranged from 20,000 Vietnamese Dong ($1) for a coffee spoon to 3,500,000 Dong ($1,600) if you improbably walked off with one of those massive rocking chairs. Carved Continental coat hangers came at a punitive $15 each. I got the impression that this hotel has been swamped by souvenir hunters in the past.

The other details were more appealing, however. A brass letterbox was cut into my door and anything posted through it fell into a small cage. My handwritten breakfast voucher was dropped in later that afternoon.

Breakfast itself turned out to be buffet-style, a delicious mix of Western and Vietnamese fare in the courtyard downstairs in the shade of frangipani trees. Birds dive-bombed the tables for tidbits. My fellow guests were about as international as you could get, with a fair smattering of Europeans and Australians backpacking their way through South-east Asia. The only part of the hotel that disappointed was the bar, which would have been more gracious if it were housed off the courtyard. Instead I found it hidden up on the first floor overlooking the courtyard (hence its nickname 'The Continental Shelf' among war correspondents, who claimed they were safe up there from any grenades tossed into the hotel).

Today it's known as the Starrynite Bar, its logo a mini-skirted Vietnamese maiden playing billiards. Not entirely clued up on modern marketing techniques, the bar proudly proclaims 'Buy One Beer, Get One Beer', which struck me as the least you can reasonably expect when handing over your Dong.

But at a time when hotels around the world are increasingly coming to resemble each other, as they compete over ever-greater levels of pampering and try to anticipate your every wish, it's rather wonderful that the Continental has not moved with the times. The Continental really could not give a rat's arse about your every wish.

That afternoon I decided to follow the route that Greene's shabby journalist, Thomas Fowler, takes in Chapter 2 of *The Quiet American*. I turned right out of the Continental up Rue Catinat (now Dong Khoi) as far as the neo-Gothic cathedral of Notre-Dame. Just across the road from the cathedral is the Central Post Office, built the year the Continental opened and resembling a cavernous railway station concourse from the days of steam. Finally I walked as far as the Rex Hotel, which is still here too, as it was in Greene's day, and the Chinese market full of over-eager traders. With its excitable merchants and omnipresent motor scooters, this is a very noisy city indeed but still the landscape of *The Quiet American*.

When I returned to Lam Son Square, I realised I was close to where Greene's fictional 'Third Force' operatives detonated a bomb outside the opera house in both the novel and the two films that have been made from it. So I quickened my pace and returned to the bar of the Continental of Greene's novel for a gin and tonic. Here you may only get one beer when you pay for one beer, but it's always been safe from explosions, fictional or otherwise. I found that oddly comforting.

NORTH AFRICA

SHARIA IBRAHIM PASHA NAGIB, CAIRO – OLIVIA MANNING (1908–80)

I never met Olivia Manning, but I did briefly meet her husband, the legendary BBC producer R.D. Smith, shortly after her death. It was in the old BBC Club (now restored as London's Langham Hotel) where in the 1980s hardboard was still nailed to the walls as a wartime precaution. Suddenly out of the darkness of the bar a big man with a very red face loomed up over us. My host greeted him, told me this was 'the legendary Reggie Smith', and the big man passed on his slightly blurred, amiable way. It was only afterwards that I realised this was *the* Reggie Smith, the model for the hyper-gregarious Guy Pringle in six remarkable novels by Olivia Manning.

The Balkan Trilogy and *The Levant Trilogy* are wonderful books for a view of the Second World War from the perspective of the middle-class European flotsam that finds itself shunted around the Mediterranean as Germany invades everywhere. Olivia Manning wrote very close to her own experiences with Reggie as they fled from the Balkans to Athens and thence to Cairo and Jerusalem. A lot of the Smiths' friends – and Olivia's personal enemies – feature, thinly disguised, in the books. The only fictional element she seems to have imported into the trilogies is the wistful personality of Guy's wife Harriet, who, if all the anecdotes about 'Olivia Moaning' are true, is a much, much nicer person than her creator ever was.

Years later my wife and I were on holiday in Cairo when I realised that our hotel in Garden City overlooked the British Embassy, which meant that somewhere nearby must be where R.D. Smith and Olivia Manning lived in the flat of Adam Watson, a diplomat they'd roomed with in Bucharest and who by 1941 was third secretary at the embassy. I wanted to see this place.

During her time in Cairo Olivia worked on *Guests at the Marriage*, an unpublished novel that covered the ground she would later explore more fully and definitively in *The Balkan Trilogy*. She also wrote short stories and poetry, some of which she sent to her friend Stevie Smith in Palmers Green in north London in the hope of publication. Not all of it arrived. Given the way the whole world was going up in flames at the time, that's hardly surprising. For her important essay 'Poets in Exile' for *Horizon* magazine, Olivia managed to smuggle it to London in a diplomatic bag.

So one morning after breakfast I walked round to find Sharia Ibrahim Pasha Nagib, an affluent wide street now known as Ibrahim Naguib. It was no distance at all. The streets of Garden City are calm, relatively spacious and tree-lined. The architecture and atmosphere of the suburb reflect Khedive Ismail's desire at the end of the nineteenth century to Europeanise his city. Here private investors built spacious homes and apartment blocks on the east bank of the Nile. Back in 1941, however, Garden City was anything but quiet. The British army was based – wholly unofficially – at 10 Sharia Tolombat, which was known to taxi drivers as 'The Secret Building' because it was supposed not to exist. Special Operations was based at Sharia Rustum where Evelyn Waugh and Patrick Leigh Fermor were doing their bit to create chaos

Photo: © David Knox

behind enemy lines, and the SAS and Long Range Desert Group were everywhere and (officially) nowhere.

If you were young enough and male it was all huge fun. David Stirling – 'the Phantom Major' who founded the SAS – convinced himself that the only way to get his big enterprise off the ground was to go to the top, so he broke into Army HQ at 10 Sharia Tolombat and managed to come face to face with commander-in-chief Claude Auchinleck (although he almost got himself shot in the process). Peter Stirling, David's brother, lived above Olivia and Reggie at No. 13 and used to hold noisy parties surrounded by captured enemy explosives.

Poor Olivia Manning, this gung-ho world was not her. Reggie, amiable as ever, made that sense of isolation worse by spending long evenings drinking at the Anglo-Egyptian Union on Gezira Island in the middle of the Nile.

On 'Ash Wednesday' (1 July 1941) it looked as if the Afrika Korps would break through and soon be in Cairo, so the British Embassy and Middle East Command started burning all documents, blackening the sky in Garden City. It's a scene that Harriet witnesses from the embassy garden: 'The sun was dropping behind Gezira and a mist like smoke hung over the river. Passing into the mist she realised it really was smoke.'

Olivia urged Reggie to take a job in Alexandria, which she ended up disliking even more than Cairo because of the bombing raids, so they moved back to Cairo. In the winter of 1941 Olivia got a job as press attaché at the United States legation, which gave her more of a purpose – and an income – but she continued writing her fiction. It's tempting to think it kept her sane.

Olivia Manning might not have enjoyed her time in Egypt, but had she been happier she might have partied more and written less. She recorded that she recoiled violently from the squalor and callousness of Cairo, but it was in Egypt that she began to question the behaviour of the British empire. This process resulted in the creation of Harriet Pringle as a voice benignly critical of imperialism when the *Balkan* and *Levant* trilogies were finally written back in England between 1960 and 1980.

The Art Deco apartment block at 13 Ibrahim Naguib still curves gracefully round the corner but it's covered with window-mounted air-conditioners today, like a plague of rectangular warts. It's mainly offices now, though the metal and glass front doors to let on to some apartments too. No one at the British Embassy could tell me where in this block R.D. Smith and his wife lived and where she developed what would eventually become the double trilogy, collectively known as *The Fortunes of War.* In 2011 the embassy staff had other things to worry about. So I returned to my hotel walking along the Nile. The image of Ash Wednesday stayed with me, however. Evidently not all the pages burned as they floated through the air, and by the end of the day peanut vendors in Cairo were selling nuts in cones made out of salvaged paper with the words 'Top Secret' stamped across them.

It really is a good job the Eighth Army stopped Rommel at Alamein.

CAFÉ HAFA, TANGIER – PAUL BOWLES (1910–99)

Tangier is one of those places that conjures up exotic images in the European and American mind and yet remains accessible. It has a long history with the United

States: in 1821 the American legation building in Tangier became the first piece of foreign property ever acquired by the US government.

Conflicting colonial ambitions in Europe led to Tangier being made an international zone in 1923 under the joint administration of France, Spain and Britain. With a population that was half Muslim, a quarter Jewish and a quarter European, Tangier was not mainstream North Africa and its freedoms attracted both artists and exiles.

Maybe more than anyone else, Paul Bowles made Tangier fascinating for several generations of Americans. The young composer – and future author – was following in the footsteps of artists Delacroix, Degas and Matisse when he first visited, but he'd been wary about making the sea crossing from France. Bowles first visited in 1931 at the suggestion of Gertrude Stein with whom he was holidaying in the hamlet of Bilignin, north of Grenoble. When the immaculately dressed and crimped twenty-year-old protested that Tangier might be beyond his budget, she replied: 'Nonsense. It's cheap. It's just the place for you.'

Though Tangier seemed to repel him almost as much as it attracted him, Bowles returned often and eventually took up residence. In 1947 he bought a house for $500 in the Upper Medina where he finished writing his first novel, *The Sheltering Sky*. Regarded by many as the definitive account of the American (and European) experience in North Africa, it was successfully filmed in Tangier in 1990 and features a cameo from Bowles himself, sitting at Café Colon in Rue de la Kasbah in its final frames.

One long weekend many years ago, I was in Tangier in the company of a gambler who had come here for the casinos. Growing tired of watching him quietly lose money, I visited the American legation to see its Paul Bowles Wing. The author's battered suitcase was displayed, covered in hotel and shipping labels of the kind that we reproduce on souvenir sheets these days. The accompanying text explained a lot about Bowles' field studies into traditional Moroccan music when he arrived in 1931.

The Sheltering Sky, despite being rejected by the publisher who had commissioned it, sums up a visitor's experience of Tangier well: the broken pavements, the importuning children, and the odours. Bowles was acutely attuned to the smells of Tangier: references to the aromas of frying meat, baking bread, petrol, sweat, urine and fear pepper his writing.

I asked at the legation if anyone knew where I could find Bowles' first house and was surprised that people knew only of Immeuble Itesa, the nondescript modern apartment block on the outskirts of Tangier where he lived from 1960 onwards. I know that he found his house in the Medina hard to heat and he occupied it less and less, even before he moved to Immeuble Itesa, but even so I would have loved to have seen where *The Sheltering Sky* was completed.

The playwright Jane Auer, Paul's wife in a long-term, highly unconventional marriage, also had an apartment in the block. In 2009, on the tenth anniversary of Bowles' death, a fellow resident erected a marble tablet that read, 'Paul Bowles American Writer and Composer lived here from 1960/1999'. But I found it difficult to imagine Bowles here. It's simultaneously too mundane and insufficiently immaculate.

So, as there was no way of tracking down the desert hotels where Bowles claimed that he began *The Sheltering Sky*, I went to Café Hafa instead, on a cliff-top west of the old city, in the slightly run-down Marshan district. Here there are beautiful views across the Straits of Gibraltar from a half-dozen terraces cut into the cliff-side. The café was founded

in 1921 and some of its blue-painted chairs facing the sea look original. I watched the waiters trek up and down the steps between the terraces with tiny glasses of hot mint tea and snacks of bread, olives and dips, and I thought of Bowles drinking tea here and smoking God knows what with William Burroughs. Many people came to see him at Café Hafa, even The Beatles and The Rolling Stones. I saw a picture of a white-haired Bowles and a short-haired Mick Jagger sitting close, but not too close together, two unconventional musicians regarding each other with interest, if not affection. In 1990 the American artist Julian Schnabel painted a large canvas with the words 'I went to Tangiers and had dinner with Paul Bowles'. Bowles and Tangier had become such indissoluble cultural markers by then.

Except for winters spent in Sri Lanka during the early 1950s, Tangier remained Bowles' home for the rest of his life. Sitting at Hafa he would have mused on *The Sheltering Sky, Let It Come Down* (his novel of expatriate life in Tangier published in 1952), as well as *The Spider's House* (1955) and *Up Above the World* (1966). At the end of his long life Bowles claimed his thoughts had turned back to music, but his last collection of verse was published in 1997, just two years before his death.

These days a new road, Route de la Plage Mercala, runs at the base of the cliff, keeping the sea some distance away. It's best to sit somewhere on the terraces where the road isn't visible and look out to sea and up to the sheltering sky. 'I have spent a good many hours busily trying to determine the relationship between Tangier and myself,' Bowles once wrote. 'If you don't know why you like a thing, it is usually worth your while to attempt to find out.'

The whole of Tangier was Paul Bowles' room and he certainly explored it in his fiction.

HOTEL EL MUNIRIA, TANGIER – WILLIAM S. BURROUGHS (1914–97)

I wasn't looking for William S. Burroughs in Tangier, but I often found myself at the Tangerinn, a temptingly disreputable bar where eventually I set the last scene of the novel I was writing at the time. The bar is still to be found under the terrace of a small white hotel called El Muniria, although when William Burroughs boarded here in the 1950s it was known as Villa Mouneria.

The hotel stands on a steep, scruffy slope in the Ville Nouvelle, with a patch of waste ground opposite it and a front door that is locked night and day – so don't lose your key. The steepness of Rue Magellan accounts for the hotel terrace and the large vacant space under it, which many years ago had been turned into a bar for dirty drinking and even dirtier dancing.

One evening it was just me at the bar, apart from two crewcut women in biker jackets on the small dance floor, so I spent some time staring at the photos on the wall, recognising images of Jack Kerouac in swimming trunks, and of Allen Ginsberg before he lost his hair and grew a beard. There was also a grinning man lying on the beach, fully clothed with his hat on. The cadaverous face leering at the camera was unmistakable. This was William S. Burroughs, guru of the Beat Generation, a man who had shot his wife dead by accident and now needed somewhere out of the way to hide – somewhere just like Tangier.

I knew that Burroughs began *The Naked Lunch* in Tangier's Café Central down in Petit Socco. He and his friends referred to the city's international zone as the Interzone, a

title that was given to a collection of Burroughs' early stories that were eventually published in 1989. I'd started *Interzone* many years ago and decided that Burroughs was not my kind of writer. His fiction is paranoid and satiric, verging on downright unpleasant, but there is no doubting his influence. Kerouac and Ginsberg followed him to Tangier and helped him turn *Naked Lunch* – a series of episodes written while ingesting a local marijuana confection known as majoun – into a highly influential piece of non-linear fiction that was published in 1959.

What I hadn't realised was that most of *Naked Lunch* was written up above my new favourite Moroccan divebar, in Room 9 of Hotel El Muniria. The barman showed me another photo, covered with clingfilm, that had fallen below the counter. Here were Ginsberg and Burroughs with Paul Bowles, the literary godfather of Tangier, all of them squinting into the sun. 'Garden Villa Mouneria July 1961' read the caption. 'All assembled outside Bill's single room post Naked Lunch.' It was signed 'Allen Ginsberg'.

I asked if I could see Burroughs' room upstairs but the barman told me it was 'privée' these days. Nevertheless there was no reason not to knock on the hotel door so I paid for my martini and walked uphill to the big locked door. The owner was a gentle and welcoming lady and offered to show me a room. No. 8 had attractive views across the terrace to the Mediterranean. I'm not sure if my poor French misled her, and she thought I wanted to book in, but we exchanged pleasantries and I noticed the door of the room that once was Burroughs' was now, frustratingly, indeed marked 'privée'. Was it just too toxic to offer to members of the public?

'I have a magnificent room overlooking the beach & the bay & the sea & can see Gibraltar,' Kerouac wrote to his wife from Tangier. 'A patio to sun on and a room maid,

$20 a month – feel great but Burroughs has gone insane – he keeps saying he's going to erupt into some unspeakable atrocity such as waving his dingdong at an Embassy party & such or slaughtering an Arab boy to see what his beautiful insides look like.'

Taking in the painted blue bedroom furniture of harmless Room 8, I remembered Kerouac describing the words pouring out of his friend in 'an absolutely brilliant horde'. This new book, according to Jack, was going to be 'the best thing of its kind in the world'.

And the room next door was where it all happened. I wish my French had been good enough to persuade Madame to let me see inside.

The next day I went to Café Central in Petit Socco, one of those French-African cafés where all the seats are arranged facing outward so you can watch passers-by on the road. The furniture was old and French, the walls painted an unfortunate pink where they weren't badly tiled. Burroughs drank mint tea here and listened to Ginsberg telling him to keep going. 'Don't be depressed. There's too much to do!'

The tea came in a little metal pot on a tiny metal tray. Burroughs described the café that inspired him as 'One room 15 by 15, a few tables and chairs, a raised platform covered with mats stretched across one end of the room where the Arabs sit with their shoes off playing cards and smoking kif'. It seemed wholly unchanged – and also wholly typical of Morocco.

What was it about Tangier that got Burroughs' literary juices going, apart from the freely available drugs? What was it that inspired Paul Bowles to write *The Sheltering Sky* and live here most of his adult life? The relationship between a writer and place is ultimately unknowable because it is so personal – but as Bowles said, it's well worth trying to find out.

POSTSCRIPT

MONK'S HOUSE, RODMELL, EAST SUSSEX – VIRGINIA WOOLF (1882–1941)

And in the end I came to Monk's House, just down the River Ouse from Lewes in Sussex.

Monk's House was originally a row of three artisans' cottages next to a forge. In 1919 Virginia Woolf, emotionally fragile and still to find her voice as a novelist, bought a house in Lewes with her husband Leonard. The couple were looking for a country retreat from London and they bought the property blind. When they discovered it had no garden, Virginia quickly found Monk's House, which, though primitive in terms of sanitation, heating, water and just about everything else a middle-class London couple might expect from their second home, did have three-quarters of an acre of garden. The Woolfs bought it at auction for £700 and sold their Lewes property for a profit. Never let it be said that great writers have to be otherworldly.

The old white clapboard house at the bottom of a narrow lane needed a lot of work. Internal walls were removed downstairs to create a sitting room (soon painted an arresting green) and a dining room and a kitchen were fashioned. Upstairs there were bedrooms and a further sitting room. Two lavatories were installed, both named after Vita Sackville-West (an odd tribute to one's former lover), and ten years later, after the success of *Mrs Dalloway*, the couple added an extension for Virginia, with a 'room of one's own' for writing, accessed from the garden and with her own bedroom above. Of course I had to come here and see the room that Virginia built.

'This will be our address for ever and ever,' she declared and indeed the couple were happy, secluding themselves away from London to write and garden. They also entertained the likes of Lytton Strachey, E.M. Forster, T.S. Eliot and John Maynard Keynes with his improbable ballerina wife. Yet it was from this house that Virginia Woolf walked down to the River Ouse to drown herself in March 1941. In one of two suicide letters to Leonard she wrote: 'Everything has gone from me but the certainty of your goodness. I can't go on spoiling your life any longer. I don't think two people could have been happier than we have been.'

I arrived at Monk's House one very stormy summer's day, having travelled from Sissinghurst through bursts of sunshine and rain. The whole 90-minute drive between Vita and Virginia's writing rooms had been delightful. It's rare, even in England, for two beautiful places to be linked by nothing but unbroken countryside, well-designed houses and pretty villages. I drove straight through Lewes and on to Rodmell, past the Anne of Cleves house where Henry VIII's fourth queen never lived. (In 1541 the house was given to the former Queen Anne as part of her annulment settlement from the king but she just used it for income.)

Monk's House, by contrast, is much more deserving of its famous association. All the furniture on the ground floor belonged to Virginia and Leonard, and everywhere there are paintings by Vanessa Bell (Virginia's sister). In Virginia's writing room there are the editions of the Arden Shakespeare that Virginia covered with coloured paper

while trying to distract herself from a crippling headache. Each has a label on its spine in the author's spidery handwriting. There was a custodian on hand to make sure I didn't touch, but, as I peered through my glasses at them, I could experience being within inches of marks made by Virginia Woolf's pen.

Monk's House is very popular with tourists, who can access its ground floors most afternoons. Unusually I'd been able to arrange to stay for the night because a room above the Woolfs' garage (formerly the local forge) has been turned into a self-catering flat by the National Trust who now own the house. Best of all, the room of one's own that Virginia built for writing in was only about ten feet away from my window as I sat catching up on emails and worrying about the roof above me, which had developed a leak that day.

It's a pretty refuge and is often taken by writers. There's a double bed, a galley kitchen and bathroom, and not much else unless you count a pile of Virginia's novels by the bedside. But the great joy of staying here is that after 5pm when Monk's House closes, you get the gardens to yourself. I waited until storm clouds passed overhead and then stole out as the birds kicked up a noisy evening chorus. The garden is divided up into 'rooms' with low walls and brick paving marking out the different sections. Leonard, who remained a keen gardener for the 28 years of his widowerhood, left the place looking wonderful.

The ashes of Leonard and Virginia are buried in a small walled section of the garden. Two elm trees had stood here which the Woolfs had named Leonard and Virginia. Her ashes were buried close to her tree (sadly it's blown down since, and twin busts of the couple now mark the spot). I'm glad to say that 'Leonard' has survived.

Beyond this memorial, an open lawn leads towards the church. Before you get to it, however, there is a wooden summer house where Virginia worked. Despite having built a room of her own at the far end of the house in 1929 – the year that she published her seminal essay *A Room of One's Own* – Virginia found she worked better away from hers, in a shed at the far end of the garden.

I peeped inside and saw her typewriter and spectacles lying on a suitably austere desk. Here she worked on her last books: *The Waves* (1931), *The Common Reader* (1932), *Flush* (1933), her one comic novel, *The Years* (1937), *Three Guineas* (1938), a sequel to *A Room of One's Own*, and *Roger Fry* (1940), a biography of her friend, the art critic and painter. The poor reception that this book received exacerbated her depression and thoughts of suicide. Meanwhile, the extra room she built on to Monk's House became her bedroom. Servants would find the floor around her electric fire littered with screwed-up pieces of paper in the morning.

Just beyond Virginia's shed is the garden gate where some time after 11am on Friday 28 March 1941 she left Monk's House and headed for the river, threw away the stick with which she walked and put a heavy stone in her coat pocket. Her body was not found for another three weeks. It had floated hardly any distance and come to rest against the supports of a bridge.

I hope it doesn't sound ghoulish to say that where a writer dies often tells us far more than where he or she was born. Virginia Woolf has been retrospectively diagnosed with bipolar disorder. She was also depressed that her recent works were not well received and that her London house in Tavistock Square had been bombed out during the Blitz.

But Monk's House does not feel like a sad place at all. In this shambling, rambling, bohemian place with its glorious

English garden and writing-room-turned-bedroom it is clear, as she herself put it, that no two people could have been happier.

THANKS AND ACKNOWLEDGEMENTS

In researching this book I have been hugely helped by the owners and managers of many properties around the world and by travel companies who have assisted my journeys across five continents.

In particular I'd like to single out for thanks the journalist Anthony Lambert, Kate Riley of Starwood, Philippe Back of the Danieli, Ivano Beggio of Palazzo Barbaro, Dr Rosa Maria Letts of Artstur, Gabriele Rigo-Titze, Cyndy Cruikshank of the Gritti Palace, Claudio Meli of JK Place Florence, Sean Smith of the Alexandra Hotel Lyme Regis, Camilla Colley and Julia Farish of Travel PR, Tony Fincham of the Thomas Hardy Society, Chloe Davison of TTC, Alex and Jack Mackenzie of the Acorn Inn, Sally Williams, Helen Davis and Alison Pritchard of the National Trust, Paul Kleian of the Wordsworth Trust, Mountain Goat Tours of Windermere, Ruth Crossley of the Elmet Trust, Robin Llywelyn of Portmeirion Village, Emma Allam of the Savoy Hotel London, Sophie Darley of Brown's Hotel, Rosie O'Brien of Rocco Forte Hotels, Laura Irwin at Doctor Johnson's House, the Society of Antiquaries London, John and Felicitas Mcfie in Edinburgh, Lauren Robertson of the Balmoral Hotel Edinburgh, Camille Maisse of Hauteville House Guernsey,

Andrew Chantrell of Old Government House Guernsey, Elizabeth Perrée of La Sablonnerie Sark, the family of Mervyn Peake, Valentino Piazzi of The Lancaster Hotel Paris, Burns Patterson of Hudson PR in New York, Maria Speridakos of Massachusetts State, Kelly Thompson of New Orleans, Mark Cave of the Historic New Orleans Collection, Antonina Kalinina, Jessica Zhang of Fairmont Peace Hotel, Polly Crossman of Mango PR, Karn Punthong of Mandarin Oriental Hotel Group, and David Knox.

I'd also like to thank British Airways, easyJet and Railbookers for help with some of the travel, and Kate Simon, for many years my editor at *The Independent on Sunday*, who commissioned a number of articles that led to my visiting various places in this book.

INDEX

of writers, artists, architects,
musicians, actors & directors

Also by Adrian Mourby

'Adrian Mourby has promptly followed up his excellent *Rooms of One's Own* with [...] stories of 50 of the world's most magnificent hotels, and the guests who helped make them famous.'
South China Morning Post

Rooms With a View: The Secret Life of Grand Hotels

Cultural historian and travel journalist Adrian Mourby tells the stories of 50 of the world's most magnificent – and notorious – hotels, from the Chelsea Hotel in New York to the Astoria in St Petersburg, from Raffles in Singapore to the Copacabana Palace in Rio de Janeiro. Many are world famous, some – like the Art Deco Midland Hotel in Morecambe Bay and the Londra Palace in Venice – deserve to be.

Every grand hotel has a story to tell, some have many. And some are living repositories of history. Those in key cities, like the Grand Hotel Europe in St Petersburg or Hotel Bristol in Warsaw, echo the major events of the past 100 years in their own story and the tales of those who stayed there.

The world's greatest hotels have provided glamorous backgrounds for some of the most momentous events of recent history – and some of the most bizarre. The surrealist Salvador Dalí once asked room service at Le Meurice in Paris to send him up a flock of sheep so he could fire blanks at them. George Bernard Shaw tried to learn the tango at Reid's Palace in Madeira, and the details of India's independence were worked out in the ballroom of the Imperial Hotel, Delhi. And grand hotels are not just about royalty and celebrity – some of their owners and general managers had a passion for hospitality and a need to control the world that frequently tipped over into obsession.

All human life is to be found in a great hotel – only in a more entertaining form.

Hardback, £12.99 • ISBN: 978-178578-275-6

Paperback publishing July 2018 • £8.99 • ISBN: 978-178578-401-9